## What People Say About *Going Around Th...*

Our church has been challenged and equipped through the vision of Around The Corner Ministries. The concept is so simple we almost overlook it. God wants us to reach out to our neighbors, build relationships with them, then use those relationships as a bridge to share the Gospel. I have had Todd share with the entire church in our three Sunday morning services. He has spoken and encouraged the men's group in a special setting. ATCM also has led six weeks of training for our people where they were given practical ideas and equipped to share Jesus with their neighbors. Cold turkey visitation is not well received in our day. The best way to reach people is through relationships. *Going Around The Corner* is a God-given and effective way to train God's people in building those Gospel relationships with their neighbors.
**Pastor Steve Scoggins, First Baptist Church, Hendersonville, NC and President of the NC Baptist Convention**

When we heard that our church was offering a class on how to witness to your neighbors, we signed up immediately. We were extremely frustrated because we felt like failures in our attempts to reach our neighborhood with the Gospel. For over eighteen years we were making no difference. The very first class opened our eyes of understanding. God is responsible to change hearts, not us. We are responsible to meet our neighbors needs as God reveals them. As we prayed, God showed us what to do. We are to start with neighbors of peace and build friendships and find other believers in the neighborhood to join us in praying for our lost neighbors. We had none and prayed for God to send some. Two other believers just moved onto our street. We are practicing how to share our story and the Gospel and are praying for opportunities to do so with lost neighbors. Our self-guilt is gone, and we are confident God will open doors and hearts. *Going Around The Corner* is an easy-to-read and follow strategy to reach your neighborhood for Christ, and the class covers all the details. We highly recommend both.
**Bill & Gail Yancey, Workshop Participants**

I started this book simultaneously with starting a new business, what I believe was God taking me "around the corner" as His witness in the business world. The study launched me into a new realm of understanding about what it means to take Christ to the world in which I live every day. And truthfully, it's a book I go back to time and time again to be reminded to "stay the course" and to keep doing what God has purposefully given me to do. It's a must read for anyone who wonders if God can use them right where they are, in everyday life.
**Connie Caldwell, Business Owner**

It's about time the church woke up to the huge responsibility living next door to us. *Going Around The Corner* is a wake-up call to us all. We have something/Someone that the world desperately needs, and this book calls us to share Him, right where we are. We used the book as a study guide for six sessions of our Life Group. And, living locally to Todd and Sheila, we had the added blessing of their leading our group through all our meetings. For groups or individuals, if *Going Around The Corner* doesn't get you out there meeting your neighbors, you must be glued to your seat.
**Mark Case, Workshop Participant**

We invited *Around The Corner Ministries* to share this outreach approach in our church. The information was Biblically-based, and easy to understand. The material focuses on one's own neighborhood. Biblically speaking, our community is our field! The rest is simple. We get out in our neighborhood, pray for our neighbors, get to know them in a casual, non-confrontational way, develop relationships with them, often helping them with any need, and we do all this to earn the right to show and share the Gospel. Working with a "person of peace" we create a community of believers in our own back yard and grow together. This model of evangelism is most relevant for the culture we live in today; it equips us to do what should be "natural" to the Christian. Our church is excited about what we have learned. Every Christian has a story to tell and this book and class energized us to do just that. If you are looking to add a spark of excitement and motivate your people to "get out and share the Gospel" then *Going Around The Corner* is for you!
**Pastor Clark Henderson, Newbridge Baptist Church, Asheville, NC**

*Going Around The Corner* is a wonderful Bible study. The study takes you through God's initial calling on your life, the awareness and obligation we have to evangelize those around us right where we live, how to start conversations and bring the lost to the Lord and ends with the responsibility we have to disciple new believers. So many studies today bring you the author's ideas with Scripture to back them up. Not this study. You will actually open your Bible and be led systematically to passages reading what God has to teach you through HIs Word. There is no doubt this study can bring revival to your own heart, your church, and your community.
**Pastor Richard Jelly, Brevard Wesleyan Church, Brevard, NC**

*Going Around the Corner* offers a fresh call to the church to return to doing in our own neighborhoods what we send missionaries around the world to do - take the gospel to the lost. The book is biblical and based on the authors' own personal experiences in their own neighborhood. It is not only a must read but also an example to follow!
**Missions Pastor Jim Russell, Brushy Creek Baptist Church, Taylors, SC**

This study has helped me renew my desire to engage with those who live around me. The study's design is easy to read and understand. Each day has a specific focus with relating scripture and questions. I have been challenged to look at scripture in ways that I hadn't before. The questions in the study helped me go below the surface level of just reading God's word and search for deeper meaning. I love that each day ended with a prayer focus that helped me talk to God about what I had just learned. Do you believe that God had a hand in placing you where you currently live? If so, this study will help you discover His purposes for placing you there. I definitely recommend this study for individuals or small groups that want to find practical ways to impact their community.
**Tina Hawk, Workshop Participant**

Todd and Sheila Alewine are a godly couple who have devoted their lives to the mission of the church and the Great commission. Their ministry and life of service to the work of God makes their book, *Going Around the Corner*, a vital source for anyone interested in reaching their neighborhood with the Gospel of Christ. The book helps Christians learn to see their neighborhood and work environment as a mission field and learn to pray for the neighborhood and for partners in reaching the community. *Going Around the Corner* is a practical guide and source that simplifies the task of discipleship and makes discipleship in the power and strength of God understandable and doable in the community.
**Scott Thompson, Vice President of Academic Affairs, Fruitland Bible College, Fruitland, NC**

# Going Around
# The Corner

**Taking the Gospel to Every Neighborhood in America**

**Todd & Sheila Alewine**
**Around The Corner Ministries**

aroundthecornerministries.org

*Around The Corner Ministries* exists to take the gospel to every neighborhood in America. Our mission is to equip followers of Jesus to engage their neighborhoods and communities with the gospel of Jesus Christ.

© 2016, 2018 by Todd & Sheila Alewine

ISBN 978-0-6927-8199-9

Scripture quotations taken from the New American Standard Bible® (NASB), Copyright © 1960, 1962, 1963, 1968, 1971, 1972, 1973, 1975, 1977, 1995 by The Lockman Foundation. Used by permission. www.Lockman.org.

# CONTENTS

# A WORD FROM THE AUTHOR

Over the course of our marriage, we have lived in two states, four cities, and seven different neighborhoods. Studies show that 11% of Americans move from one residence to another in any given year, and that people make an average of eleven moves during their lifetime. We would say that's accurate; not counting the years at college, we've moved nine times, and don't expect to move again more than once or twice until we relocate to our eternal home.

Americans move around for a variety of reasons, including jobs, marriage, divorce, or simply a desire for a change in lifestyle. But what if I told you that God is sovereignly active in every one of those moves?

In Acts 17:26, Paul tells us that God had a specific plan in mind when you were born.

*And He made from one man every nation of mankind to live on all the face of the earth, having determined their appointed times and the boundaries of their habitation.*

God is intimately involved in **when** and **where** you live. You are not living where you are by accident. God has work for you to do.

Over the next six weeks, you will discover the reason God has placed you in community with others, whether it be in your neighborhood, your workplace, or the gym where you work out. He is already at work in the hearts of others, and He desires to use you to introduce your friends, neighbors and co-workers to Jesus Christ.

Our prayer is that at the end of this Bible study you will see from scripture how God has called each one of us to *go around the corner* and share the good news about Jesus. Through a simple strategy of reaching out through prayer, good works, and sharing your story, God can use you to advance His kingdom and bring people into the family of God.

God bless your journey!

Todd and Sheila Alewine

# HOW TO USE THIS STUDY

*And Jesus came up and spoke to them, saying, "All authority has been given to Me in heaven and on earth. Go therefore and make disciples of all the nations, baptizing them in the name of the Father and the Son and the Holy Spirit, teaching them to observe all that I commanded you; and lo, I am with you always, even to the end of the age.*
Matthew 28:18-20

We believe that Jesus' command to **make disciples** is made up of two parts: reaching and teaching. We see this in the two words **baptize** and **teach**. A baptized disciple is one who has believed; the gospel has reached their ears and penetrated their hearts by the power of the Holy Spirit. This is the first step. The second step is that the disciple must be taught how to follow Jesus. He must learn all that Jesus commanded and how to walk daily in his new life.

This study provides a pattern for **reaching** (Part One) and **teaching** (Part Two).

**Part One includes Chapters 1-4**. We learn how to explore where God has put us, how to engage others through prayer and good works, and how to evangelize: how to tell our own story of conversion and share the gospel.

**Part Two includes Chapter 5-6**. We learn what a new believer must know to be established in his walk in Christ, and the purpose of the local church in equipping him to serve and become a mature believer who will go on to be a disciple-maker himself. This section presents a basis of material to personally disciple a new believer, as well as affirms the mature believer in his faith.

An effective way to lead a group through this study is to plan for six weeks to cover Part One, giving time for an introductory lesson, a chapter each week, and a final week for sharing stories, answering questions, and commissioning your group to go out into their neighborhoods and workplaces. After your group has had time to personally implement what they have learned, and experienced opportunities to intentionally share their faith, you could meet for a second session of three-to-four weeks, during which you would cover Part Two, with the intention of equipping them to disciple a new believer. Thus, you will have equipped the saints to be true disciple-makers, both reaching and teaching, as Jesus commanded us in Matthew 28.

# PART ONE: REACHING

*And Jesus came up and spoke to them, saying, "All authority has been given to Me in heaven and on earth. Go therefore and* **make disciples** *of all the nations,* **baptizing** *them in the name of the Father and the Son and the Holy Spirit, teaching them to observe all that I commanded you; and lo, I am with you always, even to the end of the age.*
Matthew 28:18-20

# Chapter One
## Exploring Your Neighborhood:  His Harvest

### Day 1 – His Harvest

For the next few weeks, we are going on a journey to learn how we can reach our neighbors, co-workers and friends with the gospel.  Our goal is to discover God's heart for others, and to make ourselves available for Him to use to share the good news of Jesus right in our own backyard.

If you say the word "missions" most likely an image of a far-off land comes to mind, somewhere remote that takes at least a plane ride to get there.  You probably think of staying in less-than-desirable accommodations, eating strange food, and being unable to understand the spoken language.  And yes, those descriptions are accurate for a lot of mission trips.

We also think of being called a "missionary" as something unique – reserved for those people who are truly spiritual and special. It's not for the ordinary person, like you and me. Or is it?

The word "mission" simply means *an important goal or purpose that is accompanied by strong conviction; a calling or vocation; it is a sending or being sent for some duty or purpose.*  A missionary is simply someone who is living "on mission."

Are we all called to live "on mission?"  Let's explore some scripture this week and see what the Bible says.

Matthew 9:35-38 – *Jesus was going through all the cities and villages, teaching in their synagogues and proclaiming the gospel of the kingdom, and healing every kind of disease and every kind of sickness.  Seeing the people, He felt compassion for them, because they were distressed and dispirited like sheep without a shepherd.  Then He said to His disciples, "The harvest is plentiful, but the workers are few.  Therefore beseech the Lord of the harvest to send out workers into His harvest."*

What do we learn about Jesus from this passage?

Jesus was _____ through all the cities and villages (verse 35).

What was His mission as He traveled through the cities and villages?

_____

_____

What did Jesus see?

_____

_____

What did Jesus feel?  Why?

_____

_____

In verses 37-38, Jesus tells His disciples that they should pray for something.

What is it?

_____

_____

Why did Jesus ask His disciples to pray for laborers for the harvest?

_____

What is the harvest that Jesus refers to?

_____

_____

Luke 10:1-2 – *Now after this the Lord appointed seventy others, and sent them in pairs ahead of Him to every city and place where He Himself was going to come.  And He was saying to them, "The harvest is plentiful, but the laborers are few; therefore beseech the Lord of the harvest to send out laborers into His harvest."*

The context of Luke 10 gives us even greater insight into the harvest.

Where was the harvest going to be, according to Jesus?

_____

_____

_____

What was special about these places?

_____

_____

_____

In John 4 we find a story that gives us even more insight into the harvest. Jesus is traveling through Samaria. Tired and thirsty, He rests at the well outside the city while the disciples go in to the city to get food to bring back. Jesus has a divine appointment with this lady, and during their conversation, He reveals Himself as the Messiah. She believes Him, and rushes back to tell her friends. In the meantime, the disciples return with food, but Jesus is no longer hungry. He tells them, *I have food to eat that you do not know about.*

Now read John 4:34-35.

What food is Jesus talking about?

_____

_____

In verse 35, where does Jesus specifically tell the disciples to find the harvest?

_____

_____

Jesus looked with compassion on people. He saw their hearts and their need. He was not a "far away" God, but the One who was coming to them – right into their own city and village, and He sent His disciples ahead of Him to prepare the way.

In the same way, Jesus is preparing us to be laborers in the harvest He desires – the souls of men and women who are like sheep without a shepherd. He desires their salvation, because He has looked upon them with compassion.

As you close today's study, ask God to show you the harvest that is right around you, and to give you a compassionate heart.

### Day 2 – God's Sovereignty and Our Mission

It is not enough to recognize that there is a harvest of souls. We must also recognize our calling as laborers and understand that God has given us a personal mission to reach others with the gospel. To truly believe in a **personal mission**, we must have an appreciation for the sovereignty of God.

Read 1 Chronicles 29.

What is the context of this passage? What is happening in the chapter?

_____

_____

According to verse 1, why was the temple being built?

_____

What was the attitude of David and the people, as they gave of their treasures? (v. 2-3, 9)

_____

According to 1 Chronicles 29:10-16, what did they realize about God, that caused this attitude?

_____
_____

David and the people of Israel understood the sovereignty of God over all they possessed. They realized that everything they had given to build the temple was simply giving back to God what He had provided in the first place.

To understand God as **sovereign** is to realize that He has all power, all authority, and all dominion over all things.

1 Chronicles 29:11-12 – *Yours, O LORD, is the greatness and the power and the glory and the victory and the majesty, indeed everything that is in the heavens and the earth; Yours is the dominion, O LORD, and You exalt Yourself over all. Both riches and honor come from You, and You rule over all, and in Your hand is power and might; and it lies in Your hand to make great and to strengthen everyone.*

List what you learn about the sovereignty of God from verses 11-12:

_____
_____
_____

God is not only sovereign over our possessions and our blessings, He is also sovereign over where we live and work.

Read the following verses and write down what you learn about the sovereignty of God. *How does this personally apply to you?*

Acts 17:24-28 – *The God who made the world and all things in it, since He is Lord of heaven and earth, does not dwell in temples made with hands; nor is He served by human hands, as though He needed anything, since He Himself gives to all people life and breath and all things; and He made from one man every nation of mankind to live on all the face of the earth, having determined their appointed times and the boundaries of their habitation, that they would seek*

*God, if perhaps they might grope for him and find Him, though He is not far from each one of us; for in Him we live and move and exist, as even some of your own poets have said, 'For we also are His children.'*

_____
_____
_____
_____

Do you believe God has placed you in your home for a mission?

_____

How do you know?

_____
_____

As you close today's study in prayer, ask God to give you a heart of praise and joyful gratitude for the blessing of your home, your neighborhood and your workplace. Thank Him for His sovereign plan in determining where you live, so that you can be a part of the harvest that is right around you.

### Day 3 – Dodging Distractions

What keeps you from accomplishing what you set out to do?  Often, we become excited about a particular opportunity or God-given assignment, only to fall to the wayside before we reach our goal. **We get distracted.**

Let's look at two distractions and how to avoid them, so we can remain faithful to the mission God has given us to reach the harvest in our own neighborhood.

### Distraction #1:  Wrong Perspective

Read Matthew 16:21-23.  According to verse 21, what had Jesus turned His attention toward?  What was His purpose?

_____
_____
_____

What was Peter's response to the plan for Jesus' future?

_____
_____

Jesus gives a very strong response to Peter in verse 23.  What do you learn about Peter's attempt to dissuade Jesus from going to the cross?

_____

_____

_____

Read Matthew 16:24-26.  In light of these verses, what do you think had become a distraction for Peter?

_____

_____

Peter's earthly perspective had become a distraction to him.  He was missing the eternal value in what Jesus planned to do, by obeying His Father and going to the cross.  He was thinking in terms of his physical life.  He loved Jesus and did not want Him to suffer.   He also misunderstood the true cost of discipleship.  Jesus was illustrating by His own life, that we must be willing to give up everything for the kingdom of God.

To avoid the distraction of a wrong perspective, we must change our focus from self-interest to God-interest.

**Distraction #2:  Wrong Priorities**

Read Luke 10:38-42.

What was Martha's concern?

_____

_____

What was Jesus' response?

_____

_____

What "one thing" did Jesus indicate was necessary?   What did He refer to as the "good part" Mary had chosen?

_____

What was Martha's distraction?

_____

_____

Martha's priorities were wrong.  She had good intentions; after all, she had invited Jesus into her home and felt responsible for the meal preparations, hosting, and serving. But her focus had become more about the event, and less about the person she was ministering to...Jesus!

As you think about your perspective on kingdom work, and the priorities which fill up your day to day life, ask God to show you where you may be distracted. Are you more concerned with your self-interests, rather than what God's interests are? Are you distracted by worry, consumed by tasks which keep you from focusing on Christ?

Close your study in prayer, confessing any distractions that may keep you from completing the **mission** God has given you. Thank Him that He hears your prayer, and that His Spirit will protect your mind and heart from any distractions.


### Day 4 – Avoiding Excuses

We are masters at making excuses! Most of our excuses come from an inflated sense of self – we are too busy doing other important things. Scripture addresses our tendency to make excuses and gives us the answer to overcoming them. Let's look at two excuses we often make.

**Excuse #1: I'm too busy with my life.**

Read Luke 9:57-62.

List the excuses given for not immediately following Jesus.

_____
_____
_____
_____
_____

Who did Jesus say was not "fit" for the kingdom of God?

_____
_____

The word "fit" in the Greek is the word *euthetos*. It has the meaning of "well placed, useful, ready for use, or adapted." In other words, Jesus is teaching that unless we are completely committed to our mission of proclaiming everywhere the kingdom of God (verse 60), we will not be *useful* or *ready* for the kingdom of God. When we allow distractions and excuses to hinder our commitment, we will become unusable and useless.

In this passage, Jesus addresses parents and friends. The one who asked to first go and bury his father wasn't simply asking to attend a funeral. He was asking Jesus to wait until his father died before committing to follow. Jesus' response seems harsh, but I believe He was simply stating that spiritual life is more important than physical life. Jesus' followers are to go and proclaim the kingdom of God, and spiritual life would result. Our physical life concerns are secondary. Likewise, the call of God on our lives supersedes the hold that our friends have on us.

Our earthly relationships with our family and friends are important, and the Bible teaches that we should love and care for our parents and be considerate and kind to our friends. But our first priority must be our complete commitment to following Jesus as His disciple. We cannot make excuses by allowing the obligations of our daily life to crowd out our mission to share the gospel of Jesus. If we find we are too busy to get to know our neighbors and fellow employees, so that we are unable to develop relationships in order to share who Jesus is, we must examine our priorities and make adjustments.

How can this principle become practical in your life? What adjustments do you need to make to make room in your schedule to spend time with those who need to hear about Jesus?

_____

_____

**Excuse #2: It's harder than I expected!**

Read Luke 10:3.

How did Jesus describe the way He was sending out the disciples?

_____

What do you think He was trying to tell them?

_____

_____

_____

Matthew 16:24 – *Then Jesus said to His disciples, "If anyone wishes to come after Me, he must deny himself, and take up his cross and follow Me.*

To **take up our cross** speaks of death – death to self, death to our flesh. Just as Peter cried out that Jesus simply could not go to the cross because of the pain, humiliation and suffering which would come, we often make excuses not to follow Christ because it is costly and painful.

Jesus said that He sent out His disciples as lambs in the midst of wolves.

Following Christ and serving as His ambassador and minister of reconciliation by sharing the gospel, is not an easy task. Many people do not want to hear about Jesus, because they do not wish to be confronted with their personal sin. Others are satisfied with their life and see no reason to examine spiritual truth or be challenged in their beliefs. Still, others may become angry that you wish to share Jesus. You may be rejected!

Jesus did not paint a rosy, unrealistic picture of what it would mean for the disciples to proclaim the kingdom of God. He was completely honest about the challenges, but He also encouraged them. It is a difficult task, but one that brings great joy and blessing.

**What happens when we overcome our excuses and eliminate the distractions to our mission?**

Read Luke 10:17-24.

Why did the disciples return with joy?

_____

_____

_____

Why did Jesus say they should rejoice?

_____

_____

_____

The disciples had learned a great secret. There was blessing in seeing the power of God! As we go out into our neighborhoods and workplaces, sharing the message of the gospel, we too, will see the power of God begin to change lives. As God's Spirit opens the eyes of our co-workers and friends to receive salvation, there is great blessing and joy!

Write a prayer asking God to show you any excuses you may be making that prevents you from sharing the gospel with your friends, neighbors and co-workers. Confess any tendency to want to take the easy path of least resistance and ask God to strengthen you with boldness and passion to fulfill your mission.

_____

_____

_____

_____

_____

_____

_____

_____

## Day 5 – Teaming Up For The Mission

We've all read studies that show the best way to reach a goal is to have a partner. Whether it's a weight-loss goal, or commitment to exercise, or just forming new habits to improve your life, having someone to walk alongside you and motivate you, as well as provide accountability, always improves your performance.

Jesus knew that we needed each other! The most important task He gave to the disciples was to go out and proclaim the kingdom of God. And He sent them out *two by two*.

Luke 10:1 – *Now after this the Lord appointed seventy others, and sent them in pairs ahead of Him to every city and place where He Himself was going to come.*

Why do you think Jesus sent the disciples out in pairs? Think about their task. What practical benefits would there be in traveling in pairs?

_____

_____

_____

_____

**How does this apply to your mission to reach your neighborhood?**

Read Luke 10:2.

What are the disciples to pray for?

_____

_____

Just as Jesus instructed them to pray for laborers for the harvest, we can ask God to send us co-laborers for the harvest in our neighborhood and workplace. Begin praying today for God to allow you to meet other believers in your neighborhood. As you meet them, enlist them in the **mission.**

\*\*\*\*

This week we've looked at the **harvest** right before our eyes. We've learned that this harvest is the unreached souls that Jesus died for, and that God has a **mission** for each of us, right where He has sovereignly placed us. We've discovered the **distractions** and **excuses** that can keep us from completing our mission.

What is the final step to accepting your mission?

Rewrite Luke 10:3 in your own words, putting your name in Jesus' command.

_____

_____

In order to accept the mission of reaching your friends, neighbors and co-workers for Christ, **you must believe that you are sent**!

**Will you accept the mission?**

Complete this week's study by asking God to do three specific things:

- Pray for God to show you the harvest in your neighborhood.
- Pray for God to give you His love for your neighbors.
- Pray for God to introduce you to other believers you can enlist in the mission.

Write your prayer here:

_____

_____

_____

_____

_____

_____

_____

_____

_____

_____

_____

# Chapter Two
## Engaging Your Neighbors Through Prayer: His Heart

### Day 1 – The Power of Prayer

> *"Self-will and prayer are both ways of getting things done.*
> *At the center of self-will is me, carving a world in my image,*
> *but at the center of prayer is God, carving me in his Son's image."*
> -Paul Miller[1]

If you ask most people who claim to be a Christian if they believe in the power of prayer, they would reply with an emphatic "yes, of course!" This doesn't mean that God has answered all our prayers! But most of us truly do believe that God is moved to action when we pray.

But how many of us believe that prayer is vital to accomplish the work of God, more than anything we physically do? That prayer _is_ the work of ministry? We talk a lot about prayer, and there are countless resources on how and why to pray. Information about prayer is not our issue…it's the commitment to actually pray that we lack!

Let's consider the power of prayer as it connects to our mission in reaching our neighbors and co-workers for Christ.

Prayer is the first step to **engage our neighbors.**

To *engage* someone in this context is to get or keep someone's attention or interest. Our end goal is that we might have an opportunity to share the gospel, by being light and salt to our neighbors (Matthew 5:13-16). But even before we engage them personally, we must go to our Father on their behalf, for it is the work of His Spirit to open hearts to receive the gospel.

Read Acts 1:1-14.

What was Jesus' last words to the disciples, just before He ascended into heaven?

_____

_____

_____

Cross-reference this passage with Luke 24:48-49 and John 15:26-27. With what "power" would the disciples be clothed?

_____

Where would the disciples be witnesses? (Acts 1:8)

_____

_____

According to Luke 24:48, the disciples were to be "witnesses." Of what were they witnesses? Look back at Luke 24:45-47 for the answer.

_____

_____

According to Acts 1:12-14, after the disciples had heard Jesus' instructions to be His witnesses in all the world and had watched Him ascend into heaven, where did they go? What steps did they take to fulfill His instructions?

_____

_____

Jesus had just given the disciples their most important task: to be witnesses of His resurrection to all the world. If you had been given a supremely important job, wouldn't you think you should immediately begin to complete the task? Jesus knew that in their human thinking, this would be the natural response. So, He told His disciples to wait in Jerusalem until they were empowered by the Holy Spirit. Their response was to gather together and pray.

So often we believe that to accomplish great things for God, we must immediately put all our talents, resources and abilities together and come up with a plan to do something. The disciples understood that the first and most important thing they could do was to pray, and to wait for God's Spirit to move.

Read Acts 2:1-11.

Where were the disciples on the day of Pentecost? What do you think they were doing? (Cross-reference Acts 1:14).

_____

_____

Describe what happened to the disciples.

_____

_____

_____

According to verse 6, what did the Holy Spirit enable the disciples to do?

_____

_____

What do you think the disciples were saying to the people?  Support your answer with scripture.

_____

_____

_____

Because the disciples were obedient to Jesus' instructions, they were right where they were supposed to be when the Holy Spirit came from heaven and filled each one of them, enabling them to speak in foreign languages, so they could proclaim the mighty deeds of God!

What do you think would have happened if the disciples had tried to speak to the people about Jesus before the Holy Spirit came?

_____

_____

_____

The story of Pentecost and the coming of the Holy Spirit is just the first of many stories in the book of Acts, where the power of prayer precedes a great work of God.  Prayer is the catalyst that moves God's hand.  Prayer is the invitation for God's Spirit to take our words, our thoughts, and our deeds, and empower them for great spiritual work.  Prayer is the work that must be done before we approach our neighbors.  It is asking God to speak to our neighbors, so that they are ready to hear when it is time for us to talk to them.

Spend some time praying, asking God to empower you and fill you with His presence.  Begin now to invite Him to speak to your neighbors.

### Day 2 – Listening To The Spirit

Unlike prayer itself, *prayer walking* is not a spiritual discipline, or a biblical command.  There is nothing mysterious or supernatural about praying while walking, as opposed to praying anywhere or anytime.  God hears our prayers whether we are at home, at work, at school, or while driving in our car.  There is, however, something supernatural about praying!

To go on a prayer walk is simply an opportunity to invite God into the lives of our neighbors.

Consider just a few benefits of prayer walking:

- It focuses our thoughts so that we can be intentional in our prayers.
- It allows us to pray for every person in our neighborhood, as we pass by their home.
- It disciplines our mind and thoughts, so we can listen to God's Spirit as we walk.
- It invites Jesus to come to our neighborhood.
- It gives us opportunities to meet our neighbors while we are outside.
- It gives us a structured, sustained method of praying; for example, every day I walk to exercise my physical body, I can use that time to pray for my neighbors.
- It is encouraging when done with a partner but can also be done alone.

Last week you began praying for a teammate, a like-minded believer who lives in your neighborhood. Prayer walking is a wonderful way to get to know a new neighbor who also desires to be a witness for Christ. Together, you can encourage one another, hold each other accountable, and pray consistently and powerfully for your neighbors.

**Let's look at a story in the Bible about a believer who was on a "prayer walk."**

Read Acts 8:25-40.

What were Philip and Peter doing as they walked through the villages?
_____
_____

Who spoke to Philip, and what were the instructions?
_____
_____

Who did Philip meet?
_____
_____

Where had the Ethiopian been? What does this tell you about him?
_____
_____

Why did Philip approach the Ethiopian's chariot?
_____
_____

What became the topic of conversation?  How did this happen?

_____

_____

_____

What was the centerpiece of Philip's message? (verse 35, 37)

_____

_____

_____

How did the Ethiopian respond?

_____

_____

_____

How do we know that the Ethiopian was truly saved?

_____

_____

What happened to Philip after the Ethiopian was baptized?  What did he continue doing?

_____

_____

_____

Although scripture does not define Philip's journey as a "prayer walk," we can learn some key things about prayer walking from his experience with the Ethiopian eunuch.  Here are a few observations:

- Philip was simply preaching the gospel as he went through the towns and villages. It was his way of life.  He met people and talked to them about Jesus.

- God sovereignly sent Philip to meet the Ethiopian.  God was already working in the heart of the Ethiopian.

- Once Philip established that the Ethiopian was open to hearing about the gospel, he kept his message focused on Jesus.

- Philip was listening to the Spirit, so we know he was living with a heart-attitude of prayer.  He immediately responded to the Spirit's prompting, and to the angel's instructions to go down the desert road to Gaza. This is the reaction of a person who is in communion with God.

Church history tells us that the Ethiopian eunuch took the gospel to Africa. We never know what great things God has in mind as we share the gospel with a person in our path!

What practical applications for your own personal life can you see in this story?

_____

_____

_____

_____

Close your study today by asking God's Spirit to prompt you to pray for your neighbors. Perhaps you are not able to walk due to physical limitations or other reasons. You can, however, go on a "virtual" prayer walk right in your own home. As you pray, picture each neighbor who lives near you, and lift them up to the Father. Write down the people you have prayed for today.

_____

_____

_____

_____

### Day 3 – Praying With Insight

Praying for our neighbors, whether by prayer walking our neighborhoods or praying from our own home, requires insight. The beauty of prayer walking is that it gets you outside of your own house.

We all have busy schedules and come home from work tired and ready to relax. Sometimes the last thing we want to do is talk to our neighbors! But God doesn't want us to live secluded, selfish lives. He has sovereignly put us where we are so that He can use us, just like He did Philip. He desires to speak to our neighbors, and He wants to use our voices and our deeds, to make His message clear.

By prayer walking, you begin to gain insight in **how to pray**. We might start out with a general prayer of "Please, God, save all my neighbors!" But as we get to know them, we can pray more specifically. You can ask God to comfort the elderly neighbor whose wife just passed away. You can ask God to heal the young neighbor who was just diagnosed with cancer. You can pray specifically as you learn the spiritual condition of your neighbors; if they've heard the gospel, for God to bring fruit from the seeds of the Word that were planted, or if they haven't heard yet, for God to give you opportunities to share the gospel.

By walking through your neighborhood, praying as you go, and stopping to chat when you meet a neighbor, you create opportunities to gain *insight.* Others have referred to this concept as praying *on site with insight*.

Paul and Silas were two people who learned to pray with insight. Let's see what we can learn from their experience in a Philippian jail.

**Read Acts 16:11-34.**

What were Paul and Silas looking for on the Sabbath day? (v. 13)

_____

_____

_____

Where were they going when the slave girl followed them? (v. 16)

_____

_____

_____

What did Paul do that resulted in their being thrown into jail? (v. 17-24)

_____

_____

_____

What was Paul and Silas' response to being jailed? (v. 25)

_____

_____

_____

Describe what happened in verses 26-30.

_____

_____

_____

What was the jailer's question? (v. 30)

_____

_____

_____

Why do you think he asked this?

_____

_____

_____

What was the result?  (v. 31-34)

_____

_____

_____

Paul and Silas were men who prayed, whatever the circumstance.  As they came into a new city, they found *a place of prayer*.  While there, they were able to lead Lydia to faith in Christ, because God was already working in her.  As they were *going to pray*, they were hindered by spiritual warfare – a young girl possessed by an unclean spirit.  Paul was aware of what was going on, because he was in a spirit of prayer.  By casting out this demon, Paul and Silas found themselves in jail, where again, their immediate response was *to pray*.

Scripture doesn't indicate that the jailer was listening to Paul and Silas' prayers and songs.  We know the prisoners were listening, but the jailer was asleep until the earthquake awakened him.  He "rushed in" after Paul called out to him that they were all still there and had not escaped.  But Paul and Silas' prayers had an effect on the Philippian jailer.  God was at work, not only to release them from their physical prison, but to release the jailer from his spiritual prison.  We don't know what they were praying, but knowing their passion for the gospel, I believe that they were praying for God to use their captivity to bring salvation to someone that night.

Paul and Silas saw the opportunity for God to work.  They had *insight*, and so they prayed *on site.*

\*\*\*

Has God ever put you in a place or circumstance that you thought might have been a mistake?  Perhaps He sovereignly chose that circumstance, so that you could begin praying with *insight* – seeing the possibilities and asking Him to work in the hearts of those you are with.

Close your study today by asking God to allow you to see your current situation and circumstance as He sees it.  Who has He brought you into contact with – a neighbor, a co-worker – who needs to hear about Jesus?  Begin praying right where you are – *on site*, with the *insight* that God gives you through His Spirit!

## Day 4 – A Person Of Peace

*Men may spurn our appeals, reject our message, oppose our arguments,*
*despite our persons, but they are helpless against our prayers.*
-Sidlow Baxter[2]

Did you know that prayer is unstoppable?

A person who does not wish to hear the gospel can turn away from us, or emphatically tell us they do not wish to hear what we have to say to them, but they cannot stop us from praying for them.

As we begin to pray for our neighbors, friends and co-workers, we can expect opposition. It may come in the form of spiritual warfare, or persecution, or ridicule, or outright rejection. The beauty of prayer is that no matter the opposition, we can continue to pray.

As we pray for our neighbors, we want to ask God to reveal a ***person of peace.*** What does this phrase mean? Let's look at scripture and see what we can learn.

Read Luke 10:1-11.

As the disciples went into the cities and villages, for whom were they preparing the way? (v. 1)

_____

_____

_____

What were they to do when they first entered a city? (v. 5)

_____

_____

_____

For what kind of person were they looking? (v. 6)

_____

_____

_____

If the house contained a "man of peace," what were they to do? (v. 7-9)

_____

_____

If the disciples were not welcomed, what was to be their response? (v. 10-11)

_____

_____

_____

A "man of peace" is translated literally as a "son of peace." It means a person inclined toward peace. The disciples were to enter a city and locate a place to stay where they would be welcomed. A person of peace was not necessarily a believer, but one who was open to receiving the message of the gospel.

Why do you think Jesus instructed the disciples to "wipe off the dust" from the cities which rejected them? Read Luke 10:16 for insight.

_____

_____

_____

_____

Sometimes people simply do not want the gospel. Their spiritual eyes have not been opened. The enemy has blinded them and hardened their heart. Jesus indicates that there will be people we meet are not ready to receive the precious truth that He loves them. In that case, we are not to continue trying to convince someone whose heart is not ready; but we can pray for them and love them.

On the other hand, God is already working in many individuals around us. These are the "people of peace" that we are asking God to reveal to us, as His Spirit prompts us to pray for our neighbors. These are the people that we will just "happen" to bump into on our walks, or just "happen" to fall into a conversation with! God sovereignly orchestrates these connections – and this is what we pray for.

As we saw in Acts 16, Lydia was a **person of peace.** She was already a worshipper of God, but she had not yet heard about Jesus. Did she "just happen" to be in Philippi, and "just happen" to run into Paul at the riverside? No! God had divinely orchestrated their meeting. He had already prepared her heart, and He used Paul to speak the words that led to her salvation.

In Acts 8, the Ethiopian eunuch that Philip witnessed to was also a **person of peace.** He was seeking answers to his questions about God. God was already working in his heart.

**Peter Meets A Person Of Peace**

Acts 10 tells the story of Peter and Cornelius, a Roman centurion. It is a great example of how God works separately in the hearts of two people, to bring them together for His divine purpose of salvation! Read the entire chapter, and then answer the following questions.

What was Cornelius' spiritual condition? (v. 1-2)

_____

_____

Who did Cornelius send for, and why? (v. 3-8)

_____

_____

What experience did Peter have before Cornelius' servants arrived at his house? (v. 9-16)

_____

_____

_____

Did Peter understand the vision he had seen? (v. 17)

_____

_____

Why did Peter agree so quickly to go with the men to Cornelius' house? (vs. 19-23, 28-29)

_____

_____

What happened at Cornelius' house? What did both Peter and Cornelius realize? (v. 24-33)

_____

_____

What was Peter's message about? (v. 34-43)

_____

_____

What was the result? (v. 44-48)

_____

_____

_____

Peter was God's messenger.
Cornelius was his ***person of peace.***

God was working in Cornelius' heart, and at the same time, He was preparing Peter to bring the message of the gospel to Cornelius.

This is what we pray for as we prayer walk. We are asking God, "*Who are you working on?*" We are making ourselves available to speak to them. And we are praying for Jesus to come to our neighborhoods, just as He sent the disciples into the villages *where He Himself was going to come.* (Luke 10:1)

Tomorrow we will look at some practical ways to recognize a person of peace, but for today, close your study time by asking God to show you the person in your neighborhood in whom He is already at work. Ask Him to give you an opportunity to meet your ***person of peace.***


**Day 5 – An Unlikely Mission?**

Let's close this week by listing some practical tips to recognize and identify a person of peace whom God may be calling us to meet.

But first, let's reconsider the story we read yesterday in Acts 10, because there is a valuable lesson for us that is easy to miss!

To review, read Acts 10:9-16, 25-29.

What was Peter's vision about? (v. 9-16)

_____
_____
_____
_____

What clear statement did God make to Peter three times? (v. 15-16)

_____
_____

Was Peter's vision about unclean animals, or something more? (v. 28-29)

_____
_____

At first, Peter did not understand what God was trying to tell him in this strange vision of unclean animals. In fact, verse 17 says he was *greatly perplexed!*

The meaning of the vision became crystal clear to him when he found himself sharing the gospel with a Gentile – a Roman centurion, who in his Jewish heritage would have been considered unclean. In fact, it was unlawful for him to even associate with a foreigner.
Read Acts 10:34-35.

What does Peter declare?

_____

_____

_____


Here's our lesson for today.

There may be someone in your neighborhood who is the very **person of peace** that God has chosen for you to minister to and share the good news of salvation with, who is a most unlikely person. It may be the last person you think would want to hear the gospel. It may be a person who is very religious, very committed to worshipping a false god. Or it may be someone who from all outward appearances has no interest at all in spiritual discussions. Only God knows what is happening in a person's heart, and the work of the Spirit may not be evident to us until we develop friendships which lead to conversations.

Peter's experience is a great reminder that salvation is for all people.

Revelation 5:9 tells us that Jesus came to purchase salvation for men from every tribe and tongue and people and nation. We must be careful that our own personal prejudices and thoughts do not cause us to miss the **unlikely person of peace** that may be the very one God is working on!

\*\*\*

## Recognizing A Person Of Peace

Based on Luke 10, here are some practical observations:

- They welcome you (v. 6, your peace rests on them)
- They receive you (v. 7, they allow you into their home)
- They serve you (v. 7, they feed you)
- They allow you to serve them (v. 9, the disciples healed; we minister in different ways)
- They listen to you (v. 9, they are willing to hear about the gospel)

As we close today, spend some time thinking about your neighbors and co-workers. Who comes to mind, as a person for whom you already have an affection and compassion? Who is your heart shaped to reach? Who is already responding positively to you? What is Jesus saying to you as you pray about this?

If God brings someone to mind, write their name here. Then pray for them!

_____

_____

_____

_____

_____

[1] Miller, Paul E. "A Praying Life: Connecting With God In A Distracting World." (NavPress, 2009) 160-161.
[2] Apologetics 315. "Sunday Quote: J. Sidlow Baxter on Prayer." June 13, 2010, http://www.apologetics315.com/2010/06/sunday-quote-j-sidlow-baxter-on-prayer.html.

# Chapter Three
## Engaging Your Neighbors Through Good Works:  His Glory

### Day 1 – Love God First

Last week we learned that the first step in reaching our neighbors and co-workers for Christ is to begin to pray for them.  We must ask God to begin His work in their hearts.  We join with other believers to pray consistently and intentionally for them.  And we listen to the prompting of God's Spirit to recognize the people of peace in our sphere of influence.

This week we are going to learn how to reach out to others through the ministry of **good works.**  We will use Luke 10 and the story of the Good Samaritan as our guide.  But before we can begin ministering to others, something must take place in our own life.

Just before Jesus told the story of the Good Samaritan, He was asked an interesting question.  Consider Luke 10:25-29:

*And a lawyer stood up and put Him to the test, saying, "Teacher, what shall I do to inherit eternal life?"  And He said to him, "What is written in the Law? How does it read to you?"  And he answered, "You shall love the Lord your God with all your heart, and with all your soul, and with all your strength, and with all your mind, and your neighbor as yourself."  And He said to him, "You have answered correctly; do this and you will live."  But wishing to justify himself, he said to Jesus, "And who is my neighbor?"*

What was the lawyer's question?  What was he seeking?

_____

What was the answer?

_____

_____

How are we to love God?  Be specific.

_____

_____

How are we to love our neighbor?

_____

_____

The lawyer asked Jesus how to inherit eternal life. He was looking for a "to do" list, an action he could take to ensure that heaven was in his future as evidenced by his desire to justify himself (v. 29). Jesus points him to the Law, and the lawyer correctly interprets it, quoting from Deuteronomy 6:5 and Leviticus 19:18.

Did you think Jesus was giving the lawyer a "to do" list? Why or why not?

_____

_____

_____

What do you think it means to love God with all your heart, soul, strength and mind?

_____

_____

_____

_____

**Loving God comes before loving our neighbor, so we must learn how to love God.**

Read the following scriptures and write down what you learn about loving God.

Joshua 23:11

_____

_____

Romans 8:28

_____

_____

1 Thessalonians 4:9

_____

_____

2 Thessalonians 3:5

_____

_____

2 Timothy 3:1-5

_____

_____

1 John 2:5

_____

_____

To love God truly is to love Him completely, with everything we are – our heart (our emotions), our mind (our thoughts), our soul (our affections and our will), and our strength (our physical bodies).

Loving God takes diligence – we are told to "take heed" to love God diligently. Love is an act of the will, a decision; it is not just an emotion, although loving someone certainly brings with it an emotional connection. Those who love God are those whom God has called into relationship with Himself. God is the One who teaches us to love others, by the way that He loves us. And loving God results in a lifestyle that reflects the character of God.

**Experiencing God's love changes us.**

Read 1 John 4:7-11, 19.

Where does love originate?

_____

_____

How do we know what love is? How did God demonstrate love?

_____

_____

How does God's love affect us?

_____

_____

What is the evidence that we love God?

_____

_____

According to Romans 5:5-8, how did God demonstrate His love?

_____

_____

What has been poured into our hearts?

_____

_____

The reason we know that Jesus was not giving a "how to obtain eternal life" list of instructions to the inquisitive lawyer is because it is impossible for us to love God unless we first experience His love through salvation. We understand what it means to love others **only** because God **first** demonstrated His love for us.

It is the love of God, which has first been poured out into our hearts by the Spirit of God through salvation, which overflows to our neighbors and co-workers. Loving our neighbors always follows loving God and being loved by God.

Have you experienced the love of God? Do you truly love God? Spend some time in prayer, asking God to reveal any areas of your life where you are not fully committed to loving Him. Thank Him for the love that He has poured into your heart. Ask Him to prepare your heart to share that love with others.

### Day 2 – Who Is Your Neighbor?

*We instinctively tend to limit for whom we exert ourselves. We do it for people like us, and for people whom we like. Jesus will have none of that. By depicting a Samaritan helping a Jew, Jesus could not have found a more forceful way to say that anyone at all in need - regardless of race, politics, class, and religion - is your neighbor. Not everyone is your brother or sister in faith, but everyone is your neighbor, and you must love your neighbor.* –Tim Keller[1]

What did Jesus really mean when He used the word "neighbor"?

In our American culture, we understand "neighbor" to mean someone who lives near us. But in the context of Jesus' command to **love our neighbor as ourselves** it simply means "the other person," or "anyone who is in front of us," regardless of their nationality or religion.

### The Good Samaritan

The story of the good Samaritan invites us to examine our love for others, our own heart-motivations, and our prejudices. It steps on our toes to ask what we are willing to do to care for others.

Let's see what the good Samaritan can teach us about what Jesus meant when He commanded us to love our neighbor.

Read Luke 10:29-37 and answer the following questions.

What happened to the man traveling from Jerusalem to Jericho?  Describe his condition.

_____

_____

What was the priest's response?

_____

_____

What was the Levite's response?

_____

_____

What was the Samaritan's response?

_____

_____

What action did the Samaritan take?  List the ways he cared for the man.

_____

_____

_____

_____

How did Jesus define "being a neighbor"?

_____

_____

According to John 4:9, why was it unusual for the Samaritan to help the man, who most likely was Jewish?

_____

_____

The Samaritans and the Jews were divided by hundreds of years of animosity. Samaritans were a mixed race of people, made up of Jewish and Assyrian heritage.  The Jews rejected the Samaritans because they had intermarried with foreigners and adopted idolatrous practices. They were despised as "half-breeds" who rejected the prophets and Jewish traditions, only accepting the Torah as scripture.

The Samaritan man in Luke 10 was moved by compassion to care for a man who most likely despised him.  He considered the man his "neighbor."  As we determine who it is we are called to love, we see three characteristics in this story that can help identify our neighbor.

## Characteristic #1:  A neighbor is someone who has a *need*.

What was the need of the man in the story?

_____

_____

_____

According to Deuteronomy 15:7-11, how are we to respond to those in need?

_____

_____

_____

How does Proverbs 14:31 say we should treat the needy?

_____

_____

_____

Why should we engage in good deeds, according to Titus 3:14?

_____

_____

_____

Do you think meeting needs is limited to physical needs only?  Why or why not? Consider Luke 5:31-32 as you answer.

_____

_____

_____

## Characteristic #2:  A neighbor is someone who has been *robbed*.

What does it mean to be robbed?

_____

_____

Read John 10:7-10.

How does Jesus refer to Himself?

_____

_____

What does Jesus call those who came before Him (those who proclaim a way of salvation other than Jesus)?

_____

_____

What is the intention of the thief?

_____

_____

_____

What was Jesus' purpose in coming?

_____

_____

_____

The man helped by the good Samaritan was in need physically – he had been beaten and left for dead; he needed medical care. He also had been robbed. The robbers had stolen his physical possessions. And perhaps we may meet individuals who have literally been robbed, and who are in physical need. Jesus said the one who loves their neighbor will have mercy and address these physical issues.

But there are also those who are suffering spiritual needs. They need to hear about Jesus. They need to know the truth of how to inherit eternal life. They need to know that false religions will only destroy them, and steal from them, cheating them out of the abundant and eternal life that Jesus came to give. To be a good neighbor, we must address both spiritual and physical needs.

### Characteristic #3: A neighbor is anyone we *meet by the sovereign will of God*.

Read Luke 10:31-33 again.

What phrases describe the way the priest, the Levite and the Samaritan came upon the man?

_____

_____

What does this tell you?

_____

_____

According to Psalm 139:1-3 and Proverbs 16:9, how involved is God in your day to day life?

_____

_____

Not one of the three men who passed by this beaten, robbed man was there intentionally. They came upon him "by chance," which simply means they were not out looking for someone to help. They were going throughout their day minding their own business, intent on following their planned schedule.

But there was one difference. The Samaritan recognized a divine opportunity to help. He didn't let his personal prejudice, or his fear of rejection, or the personal obligations of his schedule keep him from meeting the needs of the one who was hurt. He stepped into the role that God had presented him and altered the plans of his day to help.

Who do you know that has a spiritual need?
Who do you know that has been robbed of the truth?
Who have you met recently, that you know was a divine appointment set by a sovereign God?
Who is "in front of you" today?

As we end today's study, think about the questions above. Write a prayer to God asking Him to reveal your "neighbor." Who is it that God is calling you to care for and love?

_____

_____

_____

_____

_____

_____

_____

### Day 3 – How To Be A Good Samaritan (Part 1)

So far this week, we have discovered that in order to love our neighbors, we must first love God – passionately, completely, with all our being. When we love God in this way, His love spills over into the lives of those around us. Along with the lawyer in the parable of the Good Samaritan, we answered the question, "Who is my neighbor?" by learning our neighbors are those who are in need, those who have been robbed, or those whom we meet by the sovereign plan of God. It is anyone whom God puts in front of us.

Today we want to look more deeply into the actions of the good Samaritan. How can we emulate his response to a person in need, and apply it to our goal of reaching our neighbors for Christ?

## #1 – We must see with the eyes of our heart.

Luke 10:31-33

In order to care for our neighbors, we first must *see* them. How many times do we pass by people without consciously recognizing them? We throw up a hand to wave, or call out "Good morning," but we don't really take time to *see* the person.

According to Mark 8:17-21, what prevented the disciples from really seeing and hearing what Jesus was saying?

_____

_____

All three of the men in Luke 10 – the priest, the Levite, and the Samaritan, *saw* the man lying by the side of the road. But a hard heart prevented the priest and the Levite from acting on what they saw. They saw superficially. The Samaritan saw the need.

## #2 – We must feel compassion.

Luke 10:33

In order to care for our neighbors, we must be *compassionate*.

Most likely, the Samaritan had suffered rejection in his own life, so he had personal experiences that moved him to act with compassion. As believers, we must never forget what our condition used to be, before we met Christ.

Read Ephesians 2:1-3 and 11-13. What was our former condition?

_____

_____

What changed?

_____

_____

We must remember that we were once separated from God, without hope. Keeping this perspective will cause us to be **compassionate** for those who are still separated from God, and still in spiritual need. We will move from simply "seeing" a person's need, to acting on their behalf, from a heart of compassion.

---

**#3 – We must be willing to make a personal touch.**

---

Luke 10:34

The Samaritan bandaged up the wounds, pouring oil and wine on his injuries. Sometimes meeting the needs of others can be messy. We may have to get our hands dirty. The Samaritan made a **personal touch** that ministered healing to the injured man.

According to Matthew 8:3, how did Jesus cleanse a leper?

_____

_____

Leprosy was the most feared disease in Jesus' day. Those who were unfortunate enough to develop the disease were required to live outside the city and cry out "Unclean! Unclean!" whenever anyone approached them, so that no one else would be infected with what they perceived as a very contagious condition. Yet Jesus showed such compassion to this leper who asked to be made clean! He reached out His hand and **touched** him. We see in other instances that Jesus could heal simply by speaking words, but I believe by deliberately touching this man He was teaching us an important truth. We must be willing to also make those personal touches which can change a life.

---

**#4 – We must be willing to give up our own comfort.**

---

Luke 10:34

The Samaritan was on a journey, with an intended destination, and a plan to get there. He was riding on a "beast," a donkey, camel, or horse.

The Samaritan was willing to **give up his own comfort** to care for the injured man. Most likely would have had to walk beside him, giving up his own seat on the animal.

Read 2 Corinthians 1:3-7. What is the relationship between affliction and comfort? How are we to make use of our experiences?

_____

_____

_____

Paul goes on in the remainder of this chapter to describe his afflictions – burdens so harsh that he despaired of life! Yet he used those experiences to *comfort* and serve the people to whom he was sent to share the gospel. He gave up a comfortable life as an honored Pharisee, trading his position of earthly success for a life spent traveling, tent-making and preaching. He did what was necessary to care for those who needed to hear about Christ.

According to Hebrews 12:2-3, who else gave up His own *comfort*? For what purpose?

_____

_____

_____

Christ has set the ultimate example, by leaving the *comfort* of heaven to meet our needs. What could we possibly experience here on earth that would compare to what He endured to gain our salvation?

As you close your study today, ask God which of these areas you need to develop to meet the spiritual and physical needs of your neighbors? Pray over these questions and write a prayer of commitment to let God begin to develop these characteristics in you!

Do you really **see** others?
Do you have **compassion** for those you meet?
Are you willing to make a **personal touch**?
What **comforts** are you willing to sacrifice in order to share the gospel?

_____

_____

_____

_____

_____

_____

_____

_____

_____

_____

_____

## Day 4 – How To Be A Good Samaritan (Part 2)

*"There's no better way to thank God for your sight than to give a helping hand to someone in the dark."*
-Helen Keller[2]

Today we will look at three more ways that we can emulate the principles found in the parable of the Good Samaritan. By studying this parable, our goal is to allow God to develop attitudes and actions in us that make us usable vessels for sharing the good news of the gospel in our neighborhoods and workplaces.

---

### #5 – We must be willing to give generously.

---

Luke 10:34-35

The Samaritan brought the man to an inn. As the man had been robbed and had no resources to offer, the Samaritan would have had to pay for both the man's room and board, as well as his own extra expenses incurred by a detour in his journey. He, himself, took care of the man – bathing and bandaging his wounds, getting food for him to eat, and settling him into a bed to rest. Not only did he pay for the current expenses, but he reached into his pocket and paid for the future care of the man, committing to whatever expense might be incurred until the man was back on his feet.

The Samaritan *shared what he had*. He *gave his best*. He was willing to *invest* his own resources to meet the needs.

In Philippians 4:15-19, what does Paul teach us about gifts and sharing of resources? List what you learn.

_____
_____
_____
_____
_____
_____

Paul teaches us that giving from our resources to meet the needs of others is a sacrifice offered to God – a pleasing aroma! What a beautiful picture!

According to Luke 6:38, how should we give?  Why?

_____

_____

_____

The Samaritan's generosity is a great illustration that we are also called to *give from what we have*.  We are to *give our best*, and be willing not only to meet immediate needs, but to *invest* in others.  This applies to physical needs, but also to spiritual needs.

What do you have spiritually, that you can *invest* in others?  What has God done in your life?  What has He taught you?  What experiences has He brought you through?   Just as we are called to *share* our physical blessings and resources with others, we are also to *share* our spiritual blessings.

1 Peter 4:10 says, *"As each one has received a special gift, employ it in serving one another as good stewards of the manifold grace of God."*

## #6 – We must be willing to involve others.

Luke10:35

The Samaritan recognized that he could not care for the injured man by himself.  He had to continue his journey.  He did what was right at the time, meeting the immediate needs of the man, but also gave thought to what would happen to the man after he left.  He recruited the help of the innkeeper.  He wisely *involved others.*

Read 1 Corinthians 3:5-9.

As God's fellow laborers, what is our role?  Who causes the growth?

_____

_____

What does this tell us about working together with other believers to meet physical and spiritual needs?

_____

_____

Christ-followers are dependent upon one another.  Even though we are one through the Spirit of God who indwells us, we possess different gifts, abilities, talents and passions.  God uses each one of us in different ways, to accomplish

His kingdom purposes, and to grow each of us into spiritual maturity. Just as the Samaritan was wise enough to recruit the gifts and resources of the innkeeper to continue the ministry of meeting needs in the injured man's life, so we are to *involve others* as we learn to pray for, serve, and share Christ with our neighbors and co-workers.

## #7 – We must be willing to show mercy.

Luke 10:37

Everything the Samaritan did for the injured man can be summed up in this word: *mercy*.

*Mercy* is showing kindness and favor when it is not earned or deserved. *Mercy* is given as a gift. It is not giving someone what they may deserve, or what we feel is their "due." To show *mercy* is to act in compassion, putting the needs of someone else ahead of our own.

Who showed us mercy, according to Ephesians 2:4-7?

_____
_____
_____

Matthew 5:7 – *Blessed are the merciful, for they shall receive mercy.*

What was Jesus' last words to the lawyer to whom He had told the parable of the good Samaritan? (v. 37)

_____
_____

If we desire to reach our neighbors, we must be people who *show mercy.* Mercy speaks to the heart. As we exemplify mercy in our conversations, our actions, and our deeds, we will present a true picture of God's love for the unbeliever. Jesus came to show us mercy. Unlike the injured man in the story, we were not left "half dead" – we were spiritually completely dead, unable to restore our spiritual life.

*But God, being rich in mercy ...* (Ephesians 2:4). Those words should cause us to look at our neighbors with eyes of mercy and compassion and commit to be the good Samaritan they need in their life.

Close your study today by confessing any attitudes or actions which have been unmerciful towards your neighbors. Ask God to show you where you have been unwilling to give of your resources, your talents, your abilities, or your time, to meet the spiritual and physical needs of others. Examine your heart to see if there is any unwillingness to involve others in your ministry, or if you have been unwilling to be "the other person" that someone needs to come alongside them. Write a prayer of thanksgiving, thanking God for His forgiveness and His continuing work in your heart.

_____

_____

_____

_____

_____

_____

_____

_____


## Day 5 – Good Works and the Glory of God

The topic of this week's study has been how we engage our neighbors through good works or acts of service. We have learned that our first means of outreach is by prayer – praying for God to move in the hearts of those whom He is calling to salvation – praying for God to bring us to divine encounters with our neighbors – praying for other believers to join us.

As God begins to work, and to reveal who He is working in and through, we can intentionally engage our neighbors through serving them, caring for them, and doing good deeds for them. We have learned that our good deeds and service must flow out of our love for God, or we will not truly love our neighbors. We have studied the parable of the good Samaritan and examined our heart attitudes and discovered specific actions we can take in meeting the needs of others.

Today we want to look at just a few verses in scripture which speak about why we should do "good deeds" and the role they play in our mission of sharing the gospel.

Read Matthew 5:13-16.

What two illustrations does Jesus use to describe believers?

_____

_____

What happens if salt becomes tasteless?  What do you think Jesus is teaching us by this example?

_____

_____

_____

_____

_____

Where should the light be placed?  Why?

_____

_____

_____

How does Jesus say our light shines?  If the light is the glory of God in us, what reveals the glory?

_____

_____

_____

What is the result of letting our light shine?

_____

_____

_____

Jesus is teaching that our works are a revelation.  Good works are not to be hidden but are to be clearly visible by all.  The result of good works is that our Father is glorified.  Notice that Jesus doesn't say our good works are to bring glory to us, but they are to reveal the Father's glory.

Understanding the purpose of our good works – to bring attention to the majesty and wonder of God – gives us the right perspective.

What else do you learn about good works from Ephesians 2:8-10?

_____

_____

_____

_____

_____

God designed good works for us to perform, long before we were ever born. He had a predestined plan and purpose for our lives – isn't that amazing?  He called us into relationship with Him and is working out His kingdom purposes by the good works which we do, in obedience to Him.  Every time we serve our neighbors by meeting a need or doing something kind for them, we are preaching the gospel. We are laboring for the kingdom.

Finally, let's consider the attitude in which we perform good deeds for others. Sometimes we may feel burdened and overwhelmed by all the needs of the people around us. Spiritual needs are great, and if we are not walking in the Spirit of God, we can quickly come to the end of our own strength as we try to serve and care for others so that we have opportunity to share Christ.

Jesus gave us a perfect example of the right attitude for good works. Read Philippians 2:1-13 and write down what you learn from Jesus' example.

_____

_____

_____

According to verse 11, what was the result? How does this motivate you for good works?

_____

_____

_____

**Two final words of encouragement.**

**#1: Let God do the work.**

Philippians 2:13 tells us *"It is God who is at work in you, both to will and to work for His good pleasure."*

Remember that God's Spirit indwells you, and He will guide you and prompt you to every good deed. Listen to Him. Don't strive to create your own agenda of reaching your neighbors. Simply act as He speaks, and trust that His plans will create the perfect bridge to be able to share the gospel with others.

**#2: Don't quit.**

Galatians 6:9 – *Let us not lose heart in doing good, for in due time we will reap if we do not grow weary.*

God promises that "in due time" the harvest is coming. We don't know *when* we will reap, but we know that we will. Don't give up, for it may be today. God has good plans for your neighbors.

John 3:16 tells us that Jesus came for the whole world. Write a prayer of commitment below, trusting God to speak to your heart about the good deeds He has prepared for you to walk in, so that your neighbors and co-workers may hear the good news!

_____

_____

_____

_____

_____

_____

_____

_____

_____

_____

_____

_____

_____

[1] Keller, Timothy, *Generous Justice: How God's Grace Makes Us Just.* (New York: Penguin Group, 2010), 67.
[2] Keller, Helen, *Light In My Darkness.* (Steiner Books, 2nd Edition, 2000).

# Chapter Four
## Evangelizing A Person Of Peace: His Salvation

*And there was a man in Jerusalem whose name was Simeon; and this man was righteous and devout, looking for the consolation of Israel; and the Holy Spirit was upon him. And it had been revealed to him by the Holy Spirit that he would not see death before he had seen the Lord's Christ. And he came in the Spirit into the temple; and when the parents brought in the child Jesus, to carry out for Him the custom of the Law, then he took Him into his arms, and blessed God, and said, "Now Lord, You are releasing Your bond-servant to depart in peace, according to Your word; for my eyes have seen **Your salvation**, which You have prepared in the presence of all peoples, a Light of revelation to the Gentiles, and the glory of Your people Israel."* -Luke 2:25-32

**Day 1 – Boldness To Share**

Statistics tell us most Christians have never led another person to faith in Christ. Why is this? What keeps us from sharing the gospel boldly and intentionally with others? To answer this question, let's consider why we should share, based on examples in scripture of people who did share.

Read each verse below. What do you discover about why a person would share their faith?

Romans 1:14-17

_____
_____
_____

Acts 4:12

_____
_____
_____

Acts 4:20

_____
_____
_____

According to a study by LifeWay Research:

80 percent of those who attend church one or more times a month, believe they have a personal responsibility to share their faith, but 61 percent have not told another person about how to become a Christian in the previous six months. Despite a vast majority believing it's their duty to share their faith and having the confidence to do so, 25 percent say they have shared their faith once or twice, and only 14 percent have shared three or more times over the last six months.

Source: http://www.lifeway.com/Article/research-survey-sharing-christ-2012

2 Corinthians 5:14-15

_____

_____

_____

2 Corinthians 5:20

_____

_____

_____

John 3:16

_____

_____

_____

As believers, just like Paul **we have an obligation** to those who do not yet know Christ, to preach the gospel. We share the gospel because we are not ashamed, because we know it to be the power of God for salvation. This **salvation is only in the name of Jesus**. No other religion offers salvation by grace. Every other belief system is a works-oriented theology, the conclusion being that if you do enough good things, they will outweigh the bad, and perhaps God, or whatever being you believe in, will allow you into a happy eternity.

Because we have truly experienced salvation **we cannot stop speaking about it**. We may not quite know how; we may do it imperfectly and hesitantly, but if we have truly known the grace, forgiveness and love of Christ, we will have a desire to tell others. When we realize that Christ died for all, **His love compels us** to tell others of the way to salvation.

God has declared that **we are His ambassadors**, as though He were making an appeal through us. Because God's Spirit indwells us, we have a desire that others be reconciled to God. Scripture is clear that **those who do not believe will perish.** They will not experience eternal life.

We must believe these six truths if we are going to be people committed to sharing the gospel.

*It is natural that we struggle to be bold in sharing our faith in a culture that is resistant to hearing about Jesus.*

Paul was without a doubt one of the greatest soul-winners in scripture. After his conversion, he traveled the known world to spread the gospel. Yet with all his experience and knowledge, Paul asked his fellow saints to pray that God would give him boldness to speak the gospel (Ephesians 6:19-20).

Read the following scriptures. What does Jesus tell us that should give us boldness?

Matthew 28:18-20

_____
_____
_____
_____

Luke 24:44-49

_____
_____
_____
_____

Acts 1:8

_____
_____
_____
_____

To close our study today, let's revisit our original question. *What keeps us from sharing the gospel boldly and intentionally with others?*

Prayerfully consider the following questions, asking God to examine your heart. Put a check mark beside any areas that you struggle with.

_____ Am I ashamed of the gospel?
_____ Do I feel an obligation to share with others, because I have been blessed by the gospel?
_____ Do I truly believe that there is salvation only in the name of Jesus?
_____ Do I really believe that without Christ, people will die and spend eternity separated from God?
_____ Am I afraid to share the gospel?
_____ Do I believe that Jesus is with me and has given me the authority to share the gospel?
_____ Is there any known sin in my life that hinders God's Spirit from empowering me to share the gospel?

Write a prayer to God, asking His forgiveness in any area you put a check by. Then, by faith, thank Him for renewing your desire to share the good news of the gospel.

_____

_____

_____

_____

_____

_____

### Day 2 – Zaccheus: A Man With A Need

One of the very best ways to learn to share the gospel is to study examples in scripture. Today we are going to examine the story of Zaccheus. Our goal is to learn all we can about how individuals come to salvation, and how this impacts our ability to share the gospel.

Read Luke 19:1-4 and answer the following questions.

What was Zaccheus' occupation and status? (v. 2)

_____

_____

_____

What was Zaccheus' goal?  What hindered him?  (v. 3)

_____

_____

_____

What was his solution? (v. 4)

_____

_____

_____

**Zaccheus had a physical need.**  He was trying to see Jesus but was hindered by his limitations.  He was short; he was hemmed in by the crowd; and even his status as a rich tax collector could not gain him an audience with Jesus.

**Zaccheus' physical limitations exposed his spiritual need.**

According to Ephesians 1:18, for what does Paul pray?

_____

_____

_____

According to Ephesians 2:1, what is our position before salvation?

_____

_____

_____

In John 6:44, what does Jesus say must happen before a person can come to Him?

_____

_____

Before salvation, a person must have their eyes opened to their spiritual condition; they must recognize their need. Because they are spiritually dead, we know that it is God who initiates a desire in them for Himself; He must draw us before we come to Him.

As God brings a person of peace to our attention, we will recognize that He is already at work. He is drawing them to Himself. It might be in a dramatic fashion – God may bring them to a crisis, or trial that causes them to recognize their need for something or someone greater in their life. Or it might be in the still small voice of God – that inner longing for peace, for satisfaction that things cannot fulfill. As we listen to God's Spirit prompt us in praying for our neighbors and serving and caring for them, we must be listening for indications that a person's heart is softened toward God. This is the open door that you are praying for.

**Jesus meets Zaccheus' need.**

Read Luke 19:5-10.

What prompted Jesus to stop at the sycamore tree?

_____

_____

What did Jesus tell Zaccheus?

_____

_____

How did Zaccheus receive Jesus?

_____

_____

Jesus stopped at the tree because He saw Zaccheus. Here was a man ready for salvation. In verse 1 of Luke 19, we see that Jesus was passing through Jericho. Jericho was not His destination. But just as we saw in the story of the Good Samaritan, Jesus was willing to change His schedule to meet Zaccheus' spiritual need.

Zaccheus' response to Jesus resulted in salvation, according to Jesus Himself. How do we know? What two things did Zaccheus do?

Verse 6:

_____

_____

Verse 8:

_____

_____

What do we learn from Zaccheus that helps us as we share the gospel? What does salvation look like?

Zaccheus **recognized** his need.
Zaccheus **responded** to Jesus' invitation.
Zaccheus **received** Jesus.
Zaccheus **repented** of his sin and exhibited a **changed** life.

**Zaccheus experienced salvation.**

Have you experienced what Zaccheus did? Was there a day when you recognized your need of Christ? Have you responded to the drawing of God upon your heart? Did you repent of your sin? Has your life been changed?

If so, spend some time thanking God for your own salvation, and ask Him to help you share the good news with others. And if you haven't yet responded to God, why not do so today? He is waiting for you.

## Day 3 – You Have A Story To Tell

*"Have you ever wondered what it feels like to have a love for the lost? This is a term we use as part of our Christian jargon. Many believers search their hearts in condemnation, looking for the arrival of some feeling of benevolence that will propel them into bold evangelism. It will never happen. It is impossible to love "the lost". You can't feel deeply for an abstraction or a concept. You would find it impossible to love deeply an unfamiliar individual portrayed in a photograph, let alone a nation or a race or something as vague as "all lost people".*
*Don't wait for a feeling or love in order to share Christ with a stranger. You already love your heavenly Father, and you know that this stranger is created by Him, but separated from Him, so take those first steps in evangelism because you love God. It is not primarily out of compassion for humanity that we share our faith or pray for the lost; it is first of all, love for God."*
*--John Piper[1]*

Sharing the gospel begins with **sharing your own salvation story of what Jesus did for you.** When a person loves God, they cannot help but tell others.

According to Acts 4:20, what was the core of Peter and John's message?

_____

_____

Often a barrier to sharing the gospel is that we feel unqualified or inadequate. We are afraid we might "tell it wrong" or be unable to answer an important question. We feel that others who are trained in theology and evangelism are better able to present the gospel.

This is a wrong belief. Sharing the gospel is simply telling others what has happened to you. And it is telling the story often enough so that it becomes natural.

If you want to learn to play the piano, where do you start? Do you simply sit down at the piano, open the hymnal or a piece of classical sheet music, and start playing? Of course not! To learn something new, you must be willing to be taught. You must find someone to share the information and skills you need. You will start with the basics and proceed step by step to greater skills and abilities. If you are really passionate about your new interest, you will approach your learning in many ways. For instance, you will listen to recorded piano music, you will go to live piano concerts, you will read about famous pianists, you will take private piano lessons, and you will practice, practice, practice!

We understand this concept in the physical world. Why do we think that the spiritual world is any different?

How does 2 Corinthians 5:17 describe someone who is in Christ?

_____

_____

_____

According to Romans 6:4, what kind of life have we been given?

_____

_____

_____

When God saves us, He gives us a brand-new life. And we must learn to think, speak and act in new ways. Thankfully, God's Spirit comes to live in us, and He lives out His life through us. We are not left on our own to figure out this "new" way of living. But we must put it into practice (put on the new self).

According to Acts 1:8, God's Spirit empowers us to be His witnesses; so putting on the new self includes developing our ability to be a witness. As a brand-new Christian, we might not know a lot of theology, or be able to explain just exactly what happened to us. We are like the blind man that Jesus healed in John 9. All he could say was, "One thing I know, that though I was blind, now I see." (9:25)

But just as we would not hesitate to study and practice to gain a new skill, learning from others, we must also be willing to study, be taught, and practice the skill of sharing the gospel.

**Learning to tell your story.**

Just like Zaccheus, if you have received Jesus, you have a story to tell!

Think about the following questions.

What was Zaccheus' life like before meeting Jesus?
How did Zaccheus demonstrate his need for Jesus?
When did Zaccheus become a Christ-follower?
What changed in Zaccheus' life after he received Jesus?

Now, you know Zaccheus' testimony! Speaking in first person as if you were Zaccheus, write out his story of salvation:

_____

_____

_____

_____

_____

_____

_____

_____

_____

_____

_____

_____

_____

_____

_____

_____

_____

_____

_____

_____

_____

_____

Now, using the following four questions as a guide, write out your own testimony of salvation. Remember, a testimony is about how God saved you. You do not have to include every detail of your life! A personal testimony should be able to be given in about 5-7 minutes. If you do not have enough space, use a separate piece of paper.

Question 1:     What was my life like before I met Jesus?
Question 2:     How did I know I needed Jesus?
Question 3:     What happened when I met Jesus?
Question 4:     How has my life changed since I met Jesus?

_____

_____

_____

_____

_____

_____

_____

_____

_____

_____

_____

_____

_____

_____

_____

_____

_____

_____

_____

_____

_____

_____

_____

_____

_____

As you close your time today, take the testimony you have just written and lay it before God in prayer. Ask Him to use your story to tell others the good news of Jesus Christ! Commit to telling your story, practicing it with your own family and friends until it becomes natural and comfortable to you. Then be ready – because God already has someone in mind for you to share it with!

### Day 4 – Sharing The Complete Gospel

*Never lose heart in the power of the gospel. Do not believe that there exists any man, much less any race of men, for whom the gospel is not fitted.*
--Charles Haddon Spurgeon[2]

Learning to tell our own story is the first step in sharing the gospel. It opens the door. But we haven't shared the gospel until we get to Jesus. Our story is only the evidence of a changed life; *His* story is the power to effect that change.

The power of the gospel is not in our ability to speak it eloquently; it is powerful because in and of itself, it is the means of salvation. We have no power to save anyone. Only God can move a heart to respond to His offer of grace. Our role is simply to be the messenger – a minister of the gospel.

2 Corinthians 5:18-20 – *Now all these things are from God, who reconciled us to Himself, not counting their trespasses against them, and He has committed to us the word of reconciliation. Therefore, we are ambassadors for Christ, as though God were making an appeal through us; we beg you on behalf of Christ, be reconciled to God.*

According to 2 Corinthians 5:20, we are **ambassadors** for Christ, entrusted with the "word of reconciliation" (the truth that Christ came to save sinners). **To reconcile** means "to change from enmity to friendship; return to favor with."

The gospel is the story of how Christ has **reconciled** us to God. As ambassadors our responsibility is to make sure we tell His story. Very often we begin the gospel at the cross, and this is natural. But this is starting the story in the middle. In explaining the gospel to others, we want to give a "complete picture" of **why** Jesus died on the cross. Why do we need to be reconciled?

The gospel story doesn't begin with the cross. It begins in Genesis, and the entire message of the Bible can be summed up in four words, which naturally build on each other.

**Creation ⇨ Fall ⇨ Redemption ⇨ Restoration.**

---

**Creation** – We were created perfectly, designed by God for an intimate, holy relationship with Him.
**Fall** – Adam and Eve sinned, separating us from God and bringing spiritual and physical death into our world.
**Redemption** – Jesus, God's Son, came into our world as a human baby, lived a perfect, sinless life and died on the cross to pay our sin debt, and was raised up from the grave, defeating death and giving us new life.
**Restoration** – Jesus' death and resurrection restores us (reconciles us) back to God, to our original design. We are restored spiritually now, and one day we will enjoy eternity with physically restored bodies, to live in the presence of God forever.

---

Let's consider each of these four words in scripture.

**Creation:**

Read Genesis 1 and 2. Give special attention to 1:26-31 and 2:7.

What do you observe about God's creation of Adam & Eve? How were they originally created? What instructions did He give them?

_____

_____

_____

_____

_____

_____

_____

In the beginning, God created man and woman, breathed His Spirit into them, and placed them in a perfect environment. They did not know sin. They did not know good from evil; they only knew God in His perfect holiness and had perfect intimacy with Him. God gave them the responsibility to tend the garden, and care for the animals. Their only job was to enjoy Him and His creation. He gave them one rule: *Do not eat of the tree of the knowledge of good and evil.*

Sadly, Adam and Eve chose not to listen to God. The account of their disobedience is called the **Fall**.

## Fall:

Read Genesis 3. What life-changing decision did the man and woman (Adam and Eve) make? How did this affect their life? What was the result?

_____

_____

_____

_____

_____

_____

In Genesis 3:15, God promises that the woman's seed will one day bruise (crush) the serpent's (Satan's) head. What do you think this means?

_____

_____

_____

Adam and Eve disobeyed God and brought sin into the world. God's Spirit left them, leaving them to suffer physical and spiritual death. Sin brought death into the world. They were forced to leave the perfect garden and were separated from the continual presence of God. Their children would now be born in their image, rather than in the perfect image of God.

According to Romans 5:12, what effect did Adam's sin have on the world?

_____

_____

Because of Adam's sin, all men are born separated from God. We are all in need of redemption. According to Romans 3:23, *all have sinned.* Romans 6:23 tells us that *the wages of sin is death, but the gift of God is eternal life through Jesus Christ our Lord.* Our sin-need brings us to the understanding that we need **redemption.**

### Redemption:

Read 1 Corinthians 15:1-4. List the three main points of the gospel, according to Paul.

_____

_____

_____

Christ's death on the cross, His burial, and His resurrection are the heart of the gospel. From beginning to end, scripture points to Jesus, and why He came to earth: to die on a cross, to be buried, and to be raised again. The gospel centers in Jesus and His work on the cross.

According to Romans 5:6-10, why did Jesus die?

_____

_____

_____

Romans 10:9-10 tells us how we are saved. Write out these verses in your own words.

_____

_____

_____

_____

_____

_____

_____

Believers not only have the hope that comes from redemption, the reconciliation to God through the payment of our sins through Christ's death, but we have the hope of **restoration.** One day, God's kingdom will be restored.

## Restoration:

Read 2 Corinthians 5:17-21 and Galatians 2:20. What happens to someone when they become a Christ-follower? Describe their new life.

_____

_____

_____

How does Romans 6:4-11 tell us that we are to walk? What no longer has power over the believer? What does this tell you about a person's relationship with God after salvation?

_____

_____

_____

We know that God has accepted Christ's death on the cross as payment for our sins because of the resurrection. Jesus defeated death, and in Christ we now have a new life on earth, to walk in fellowship and intimacy with God, and the promise of eternal life when we die. One day, all of creation will be restored!

According to 1 Corinthians 15:50-58, to what events can a believer look forward?

_____

_____

_____

_____

_____

Romans 8:18-23 promises redemption of our physical bodies and the creation. According to verse 18, what is yet to be revealed to us?

_____

_____

_____

Finally, read Revelation 21:1-7. What is being described? Who will inherit?

_____

_____

_____

_____

_____

_____

These are but a few scriptures that give us just a glimpse into the restoration that God promises will one day be a reality. Because of what Jesus did on the cross, all pain and death and sorrow will be ended, and Jesus will take His rightful place on the throne of His kingdom. Those who are saved will inherit the blessings of this kingdom.

As you have opportunities to begin sharing the gospel story with the people of peace in your neighborhood or workplace, remember to share the complete story. As you learn and study scripture for yourself, you will become more comfortable in telling the story of the Creation, the Fall, Redemption and the Restoration of the kingdom.

Use the last part of your study today to write out the story of **Creation, Fall, Restoration** and **Redemption**, in your own words. How can you share this with someone today?

_____
_____
_____
_____
_____
_____
_____
_____
_____
_____
_____
_____
_____
_____
_____
_____
_____
_____
_____
_____
_____
_____
_____
_____
_____
_____
_____
_____

## Day 5 – Turning the Conversation to Christ

*We email, Facebook, tweet and text with people who are going to spend eternity in either heaven or hell. Our lives are too short to waste on mere temporal conversations when massive eternal realities hang in the balance. Just as you and I have no guarantee that we will live through the day, the people around us are not guaranteed tomorrow either. So let's be intentional about sewing the threads of the gospel into the fabric of our conversations every day, knowing that it will not always be easy, yet believing that eternity will always be worth it.*
— David Platt[3]

This week we've spent a lot of time studying the gospel. We've seen from scripture that sharing the gospel is a command, and that we are to be bold and intentional. We've looked at a conversion experience, discovering what is necessary for a person to accept the gospel, and indicators of someone who might be ready to hear. We're learning to tell our own story of how we met Jesus. And we've reviewed briefly the "big picture" of the gospel, the thread of redemption that is woven throughout the pages of the Bible.

So, we're ready to share the gospel!

Turning a conversation to spiritual things is an art, and some people seem naturally gifted to do just that. But it's also something that can be learned and practiced. Let's look at just a few scriptures that will give us insight into how to bring the gospel into our daily conversations.

Read Colossians 4:2-6. What was Paul's strategy to sharing the gospel? List each point you find.

_____
_____
_____
_____
_____
_____
_____

Paul prayed for opportunities to share. He prayed for clarity in his words. He also desired to make the most of every opportunity, so every conversation would be seasoned with grace – words that would draw the listener towards God, rather than push him away.

Developing the "art" of conversational evangelism is simply walking in the Spirit, listening to His prompting, and truly being interested in the person you are speaking with. It is trusting in God to lead your thoughts and your words.

**Jesus teaches us a simple strategy.**

Jesus was the master at turning conversations to the kingdom of God. In His encounter with the woman at the well, we can identify a simple strategy for moving conversations toward the gospel.

**Surface** questions lead to
      **Personal** questions, which lead to
            **Religious** questions, which lead to
                  **Spiritual** questions, which lead to
                        The **Gospel**!

Read John 4:1-42.

Why was Jesus in Samaria? (v. 1-4)

_____

_____

What was Jesus' condition? (v. 5-8)

_____

_____

Who did Jesus meet at the well? What did He ask? (v. 7)

_____

_____

_____

Why was this unusual? (v. 9)

_____

_____

_____

Jesus' first words to the woman were simple. He connected with her in conversation using the reason she was at the well – to draw water. He drew her into conversation by crossing cultural barriers. She was a Samaritan, and a woman. A Jewish rabbi would not ordinarily speak to such a person.

What was Jesus' response to the woman's surprised attitude that He would speak to her? (v. 10)

_____

_____

_____

Jesus immediately drew a spiritual connection to the subject of water. He made a statement that caused her to be curious. He was less interested in the actual quenching of His thirst, and more interested in drawing her into a conversation about spiritual things.

Jesus' statement in verse 10 caused the woman to reveal something about herself. What did she reveal in verse 11-12?

_____

_____

_____

The woman asked Jesus if he was greater than Jacob. The patriarchs were held in highest esteem by all Jews. The woman revealed that she knew something of the spiritual heritage of the Jewish nation and considered herself a part of it.

Jesus engaged the woman's religious question. What did He offer the woman? What was her response? (v. 13-15)

_____

_____

_____

_____

At this point, the woman's answer revealed that she was still thinking in physical terms. She did not yet understand the meaning of Jesus' words. So, Jesus does something unusual. He seems to suddenly change the topic of conversation to something completely irrelevant.

What did Jesus ask the woman to do? (v. 16)

_____

_____

What was her response? (v. 17)

_____

_____

What did Jesus reveal about Himself, in His answer to the woman's statement that she had no husband? What did He reveal about the woman? (v. 17-19)

_____

_____

_____

Jesus turned the conversation to a topic that He knew would expose her need, as well as give opportunity to reveal Himself as Messiah. By His supernatural knowledge of her situation, the woman's eyes were opened to accept that He was speaking of more than physical water.

What did Jesus lead the woman to discuss? (v. 20-24)

_____

_____

Finally, what did Jesus reveal about Himself to the woman? (v. 25-26)

_____

_____

Jesus began with a **surface** question; He asked for a drink of water. The conversation about water led to a **personal** question about her husband. Jesus' interest in her personal life led to a **religious** discussion: Jews and Samaritans worship differently. The religious discussion allowed Jesus to move to the **spiritual** issue in question: He revealed Himself as Messiah.

**Some practical observations.**

This encounter has many spiritual lessons, but here are a few observations of the way Jesus engaged the woman and led the conversation.

1. Be prepared to engage conversations at the most unlikely times. Jesus was tired, hot, thirsty and hungry. Yet He saw the woman at the well and engaged her because her spiritual need was greater than His physical need.

2. Ask for someone's help or ask them a question. When we make ourselves vulnerable, we are letting them know we are open to conversation. Most people are willing to offer a hand or answer a question or meet a simple need.

3. Look for spiritual connections to the topic at hand. Use whatever has connected you with this person to introduce spiritual things. It can be a reference to church, a scripture that applies to the situation, or a simple remark on the goodness of God.

4. Be sincerely interested in the person you are speaking to. Jesus mentioned the woman's husbands because He knew it would be a way to reveal Himself as having supernatural knowledge. But it ultimately showed that He cared about her as a person. He was letting her know that even though He knew she was not a morally pure person, He was still interested in telling her about the kingdom of God. People need to know we care about them.

5. Be interested in the person's spiritual beliefs. Ask questions. Never belittle, mock or scorn someone because they do not believe as you do. Use what they are willing to share about their beliefs as a bridge to introduce the gospel and the truth of scripture. If we want others to listen to us, we must be willing and interested in what they have to say as well. Jesus did not force the woman to believe. He simply presented the truth.

There are many great resources on how to share. In the appendix of this study, we have listed several online articles which give excellent practical ideas on turning conversations toward the gospel. In addition, there is an expanded explanation of the four types of questions Jesus used in leading the woman to salvation.

As we end this week of study on the gospel, consider Paul's plea to the believers:

Romans 12:1-2 – *Therefore, I urge you, brethren, by the mercies of God, to present your bodies a living and holy sacrifice, holy and acceptable to God, which is your spiritual service of worship. And do not be conformed to this world, but be transformed by the renewing of your mind, so that you may prove what the will of God is, that which is good and acceptable and perfect.*

Spend some time in prayer presenting yourself to Him as a servant of the gospel. Tell Him of your desire to be a bold and effective witness and commit to doing whatever necessary to learn and practice the art of sharing your faith with your neighbors and co-workers.

---

[1] Piper, John. *Let The Nations Be Glad! The Supremacy of God in Missions.* (Michigan: Baker Academic, Baker Book House Company, 2004), 42.

[2] Spurgeon, C.H. *Spurgeon's Sermons, Eighth Series, Works of the Rev. C.H. Spurgeon.* (Sheldon & Company, 1871), 244.

[3] Platt, David. *Follow Me: A Call To Die. A Call To Live.* (Illinois: Tyndale House Publishers, 2013), 187.

# PART TWO: TEACHING

*And Jesus came up and spoke to them, saying, "All authority has been given to Me in heaven and on earth. Go therefore and **make disciples** of all the nations, baptizing them in the name of the Father and the Son and the Holy Spirit, **teaching** them to observe all that I commanded you; and lo, I am with you always, even to the end of the age.*
Matthew 28:18-20

# Chapter Five
## Establishing New Believers In The Faith: His Disciple

### Day 1 – Rooted

*When a person makes a confession of faith and is never taken through a formal discipleship process, there is little hope of seeing genuine spiritual transformation.*
-- Dr. Howard Hendricks[1]

Read John 3:3. What physical experience does Jesus use to explain what happens when a person comes to faith in Christ?

_____
_____

What does the phrase "born again" mean to you?

_____
_____
_____

Imagine giving birth to a healthy eight-pound baby boy. Then imagine taking the baby home, laying him on the kitchen table, and explaining to him that he would now need to care for himself! He would be responsible to find and fix his own food, dress himself, and get himself to bed. He would need to learn everything about being a human being, but without any help.

"What a ludicrous thing to imagine!" you say. But isn't it what we often do to "baby" believers? We welcome them into our family but leave them to fend for themselves in learning to live as Christ-followers. What a tragedy!

When we lead a person to Christ, we must also accept the responsibility of helping them to grow in their faith. We must take seriously our obligation to **establish** them on a firm foundation of spiritual truth.

Consider our key verse for this week's study:

Colossians 2:6-7 – *Therefore as you have received Christ Jesus the Lord, so walk in Him, having been firmly rooted and now being built up in Him and established in your faith, just as you were instructed, and overflowing with gratitude.*

What is the command in this verse?

_____

_____

After a person comes to know the Lord in salvation, the goal is to learn to walk in Him.

The word "walk" refers to our way of life. It speaks of the pattern of our behavior, our lifestyle. At salvation, the Holy Spirit comes to indwell the believer. Our spirit is now alive to God, and we have a new source of power to live.

According to Galatians 2:20, how do our lives change after salvation?

_____

_____

_____

As a new believer, these changes can be difficult to understand. We have different desires but are not sure exactly how to live as a Christian. Without proper instruction and encouragement, a new believer can spend years struggling to grow in their faith.

Leading someone to Christ is just the beginning of carrying out the Great Commission to make disciples. We must be committed to help the new believer to establish a strong foundation in the basic faith principles of the Christian life. This is vital to his successful growth and spiritual maturity.

Read Colossians 2:6-7 again. Paul uses four words (verbs) to describe a person who has received Christ Jesus. List those here.

_____

_____

_____

_____

Look up the following words and explain each in your own words. Use the definitions in the shaded area below to help.

Rooted

_____

_____

_____

_____

Built up

_____
_____
_____
_____

Established

_____
_____
_____
_____

Instructed

_____
_____
_____
_____

---

**Rooted** (4492) *rhizoō* - to cause to strike root, to strengthen with roots, to render firm, to fix, establish, cause a person or a thing to be thoroughly grounded; to cause to take root.

**Built up** (2026) *epoikodomeō* – to build upon; figuratively in the New Testament, to finish the structure of which the foundation has already been laid, i.e., to give constant increase in Christian knowledge and in a life conformed thereto (Thayer's Greek Lexicon).

**Established** (950) *bebaioō* – to make firm, establish, confirm, make sure; make secure

**Instructed** (1321) *didaskō* – to teach, to hold discourse with others in order to instruct them, to impart instruction, to instill doctrine into one.

*Source: www.blueletterbible.org*

---

The word "rooted" in the original Greek is written in the perfect tense. The perfect tense represents an action that was completed in the past but has continuing results.

In contrast, the words "built up" and "established" are written in the present tense. The present tense expresses continuous or repeated action. "Instructed" is written in the Greek aorist tense, which is used for simple, undefined action. It relates less to time and expresses the reality of the event or action.

What can we learn from this?

The ability to fulfill the command in Colossians 2:6, **walk in Him,** is directly related to verse 7. We must first be rooted, or thoroughly grounded. This should happen as the natural next step after salvation. This "grounding" in our faith has continuing results, as we are continually built up and established. Instruction happens throughout our Christian life, as we daily learn from our study of the Word, from reading solid Christian material, and as we hear biblical teaching.

The process of discipleship begins with salvation, but it doesn't end there. A new believer must put down deep roots, so they can begin to grow. They must be confirmed in the assurance of their faith. As they begin to build on this foundation, they will become established and secure. And all of this takes place in the context of relational teaching. One believer teaching another believer, who in turn instructs the one coming behind them.

Who established you in the faith? Who was instrumental in teaching you how to live as a Christ-follower? Think of those people in your life who have helped to disciple you, and list them below. Then spend some time thanking God for them.

_____
_____
_____
_____
_____


**Day 2 – Biblical Examples of Disciple-Makers**

If we only had the command of Colossians 2:6-7, we would have enough evidence that personal discipleship is a biblical principle. Scripture confirms this idea in many other verses, and not least in the examples of the saints we read about in the Bible, in both the Old and New Testaments.

Read each of the following scriptures. Fill in the chart on the following page. Look for the relationships between the believers and how they taught and encouraged one another. If you need more context, read the scriptures before and after the passages mentioned.

Acts 9:26-27                    Acts 11:19-26
Acts 12:24-25                   Acts 18:24-28
Acts 14:21-23                   Philippians 4:9
1 Timothy 1:1-7                 2 Timothy 2:2

| Who was the teacher or mentor? | Who was the disciple or learner? | What was taught or modeled? |
| --- | --- | --- |
| | | |
| | | |
| | | |
| | | |
| | | |
| | | |
| | | |
| | | |

Summarize what you learned from the examples above.

_____

_____

_____

_____

_____

_____

_____

_____

_____

Close your study time by asking God to show you any areas in your own spiritual life that you need a mentor or teacher. Commit to be a life-long disciple.

## Day 3 – An Intimate Look At Personal Discipleship

*Radical obedience to Christ is not easy... It's not comfort, not health, not wealth, and not prosperity in this world. Radical obedience to Christ risks losing all these things. But in the end, such risk finds its reward in Christ. And He is more than enough for us.*
– David Platt[2]

Commitment to Christ is not an easy path.

In Matthew 10, Jesus describes the cost of true discipleship. He uses the analogy of a sheep among wolves, and warns the disciples they will face scourging, betrayal, hatred, rejection, persecution, and death. These are all things that Christ Himself faced.

Jesus tells us the goal of discipleship in Matthew 10:24-25. Write it here:

_____

_____

When a person becomes a Christ-follower, they begin a life-long journey to become like the Teacher. It is a hard journey, but a blessed one! As we commit to **establishing** new believers in the faith, we must count the cost of true discipleship. Personally investing in someone's spiritual growth does not just impact the new believer. It will change our heart as well.

The Apostle Paul understood what it meant to follow Christ. He was well-acquainted with personal hardship. Let's consider a passage of scripture that gives us insight into Paul's heart for believers.

Read 1 Thessalonians 2:1-12.

How did Paul view his responsibility to share the gospel? (v. 4)

_____

_____

Paul mentioned two kinds of relationships to illustrate how he felt about the new believers. What were they? (v. 7-8, 11)

_____

_____

How did Paul behave toward the believers? (v. 9-10)

_____

_____

What words did Paul use to describe his interactions with the believers? (v.11)

_____

_____

What was the end goal Paul had in mind for the believers? (v. 12)

_____

_____

This passage gives us an intimate look at the relationship created between a person who shares the gospel and the person who receives the gospel. They become a family. When we lead someone to Christ, their spiritual well-being should matter to us. Just as they are born into the family of God and become children of God, they also become our spiritual children. We are to care deeply for them and be willing to invest ourselves in seeing them grow into Christ-likeness.

In 1 Thessalonians 2:13-20, Paul describes his joy in the believers. He desires to come to them, to see how they are doing, yet is prevented from visiting. He knows they are suffering persecution, and his heart is moved for them.

Read 1 Thessalonians 3:1-13.

Who did Paul send to visit the church at Thessalonica, and why? (v. 2-3)

_____

_____

What was Paul concerned about? (v. 4-5)

_____

_____

What news did Timothy bring back to Paul? (v. 6)

_____

_____

How does this affect Paul? (v. 7-10)

_____

_____

_____

What did Paul pray for the believers? (v. 10-13)

_____

_____

_____

In this passage we see that Paul communicated several things to the believers.

- He desired to **strengthen** and **encourage** the believers' faith. (v. 2)
- He warned against the **deception** of discouragement, knowing that they would be tempted to fall away from the faith amid persecution. (v. 3-5)
- He desired them to **stand firm** in the Lord. (v. 8)
- He wanted to **complete** what was lacking in their faith. (v. 10)
- He prayed for their **love** to increase for others. (v. 12)
- He desired for them to be **established** in holiness. (v. 13)

Paul's intimate care and passion for the believers illustrates the kind of relationships that we must be willing to develop as we lead people to Christ. If we ourselves are not able to disciple a person personally, we must connect them with others who can.

In verses 7 and 8, Paul expresses that his own faith was strengthened in his distress and affliction by seeing the growing faith of the believers who had come to Christ under his ministry. This is the beauty of discipleship. As we invest in others, our own faith deepens and we ourselves are established. As we strengthen and encourage others, we are encouraged and strengthened.

Remember Jesus' words in Matthew 10? Let's take seriously our responsibility to help new believers face the challenges of following Christ. As you close your study today, consider praying the words of Paul's prayer over your own life, and for those younger believers God has placed in your life. Pray that God will give you the commitment and willingness to become intimately involved in helping others grow to maturity in Christ.

*May the Lord cause you to increase and abound in love for one another, and for all people.*

*May the Lord establish your hearts without blame in holiness before our God and Father.*

### Day 4 – What A Believer Needs To Know About Loving God

The purpose of this Bible study has been to inspire and challenge you to carry out the Great Commission in your own neighborhood. Our topic this week, *Establishing New Believers in the Faith,* comes out of one phrase in Matthew 28:18-20.

*Go therefore, and make disciples of all the nations, baptizing them in the name of the Father and the Son and the Holy Spirit, teaching them to observe all that I commanded you; and lo, I am with you always, even to the end of the age.*

What do you think Jesus meant when He instructed the disciples to *teach them to observe all that I commanded you*?

_____

_____

_____

How do we teach others to **observe**?

The Greek word translated as "observe" is *tēreō*, and means "to attend to carefully, to take care of, to guard." It is not our responsibility to teach new believers everything they need to know for the rest of their Christian life. We are simply commanded to teach them to **observe** what Jesus says. By our words of instruction and the example of our lives, we teach others how to respond to God's claim on their life: a life-long habit of listening and obedience.

It will help us discern what it means to listen and obey by considering the first commandments God gave to the children of Israel.

Read Exodus 20:1-17. Using the blanks below, list each commandment. Indicate whether the commandment refers to our relationship with God, or our relationship with others, by checking the appropriate box.

# 1 _____     □ God  □ Others
# 2 _____     □ God  □ Others
# 3 _____     □ God  □ Others
# 4 _____     □ God  □ Others
# 5 _____     □ God  □ Others
# 6 _____     □ God  □ Others
# 7 _____     □ God  □ Others
# 8 _____     □ God  □ Others
# 9 _____     □ God  □ Others
#10 _____     □ God  □ Others

According to Matthew 22:35-40, what two commands did Jesus give?

We are to _____ God.
We are to _____ others.

Jesus took the entire Old Testament, the Law and the Prophets, and summed it up in two basic commands: *Love the Lord God, and love others.* As new believers learn to love God and love others, they will develop a life-long habit of **observing** all that Jesus commanded.

In order to learn to love God, there are some basic scriptural truths that need to be discovered. Here are just a few. The scriptures referenced are not intended to be a study of each topic. They are provided here simply to illustrate the importance of each subject to our Christian life.

**A New Believer Needs to Know They Are Saved**

It's not unusual for a believer to doubt their conversion. Salvation is a spiritual experience, but we still live in a physical world, with natural, fleshly desires and habits. It takes time for a person to grow and change, and sometimes along the way we can suffer from doubt, questioning if God really did His redeeming work in our heart. It is very important for a new believer to see and believe the truth about their salvation, based on the facts of scripture, rather than their feelings.

Read each scripture below and explain why it is important for a new believer to have full assurance of their salvation. What are the benefits of a confident faith? What happens when we doubt?

1 John 5:11-13

_____
_____
_____

Colossians 2:2-3

_____
_____
_____

James 1:5-8

_____
_____
_____

Hebrews 10:19-25

_____
_____
_____

## A New Believer Needs to Know Who God Is

Each of us comes to Christ with a heritage. It may be a godly heritage, raised in a Christian home and brought up in church. Or we may come to Christ not ever having read the Bible and knowing very little about the God to whom we've given our lives. In either case, to truly worship God as He is, we must set aside our ideas of God and learn to know Him as He has revealed Himself to us in scripture. We must know God to worship God.

According to each scripture below, why is it important for a new believer to study the character and attributes of God? Why do we need to know God?

Isaiah 55:8-9

_____
_____
_____

1 Samuel 15:29

_____
_____
_____

Psalm 46:10

_____
_____
_____

Proverbs 9:10

_____
_____
_____

## A New Believer Needs to Communicate With God

At salvation, a new believer enters into an intimate relationship with God. Just like any relationship, this needs to be cultivated and nurtured. For the Christ-follower, this happens through hearing God speak in His Word, and speaking back to Him in prayer.

The habit of Bible study and the practice of prayer is first learned in the context of a local church. We'll discuss these two spiritual disciplines more in the next chapter. For today, read each scripture below. Does it refer to God's Word, or prayer? What practical benefits do you see from each scripture?

John 8:31-32

_____

_____

_____

Psalm 19:7-11

_____

_____

_____

Psalm 119:165

_____

_____

_____

1 Thessalonians 5:16-18

_____

_____

_____

John 16:23-24

_____

_____

_____

Hebrews 4:16

_____

_____

_____

Loving the Lord begins with the assurance of our salvation. We must know confidently that we are in a covenant relationship with God, accepted by grace, through faith. Only then can we begin to learn about God Himself. As we learn to study His Word and commune with Him in prayer, we will discover who He is – His attributes and His character. As we learn to listen to the Spirit's voice in us, we will begin to understand this new life in Christ – Christ in us, working out His plan and purpose, for His glory. These are the foundations of a new believer's love for the Lord.

As you end today's study, think about your own love for the Lord. Remember – it is out of our love for God that we can love others and see them with eyes of compassion. Spend some time in prayer telling God how much you love Him.

## Day 5 – What A Believer Needs to Know About Loving Others

As we saw yesterday, a new believer needs to learn what it means to **love God** and **love others.** Starting our new life with Christ with a confident assurance of our salvation sets us onto a path of communicating with Him through prayer and His word, and learning more about Him each day, and growing in intimacy with Him.

As we develop our vertical relationship with God, then our horizontal relationships with others start to change. We begin to learn what it means to **love others.**

Ephesians 4:16 refers to the body of Christ. Next week we will study this in depth, but for now, how does this verse say the body builds itself up?

_____

_____

_____


New believers must be taught the importance of fellowshipping with other believers. God brings us into a family. We are all adopted by God, and it is the context of the family of Christ that we learn how to love one another.

We love others by letting God's Word guide our actions, words and attitudes. His Word influences our **obedience to God** and our ability to **handle temptation.** We also love others by being willing to **share the gospel** with unbelievers.

### A New Believer Must Learn to Obey God

Why is obedience important? According to these scriptures, what are the practical benefits of obedience to God? What place does obedience have in the believer's life?

John 3:36

_____

_____

_____

James 4:17

_____

_____

_____

1 Peter 1:13-16

_____

_____

_____

## A New Believer Must Learn How to Handle Temptation

Once we become part of God's family, sin no longer has the *power* to separate us from God. Christ's sacrifice on our behalf covers all our sins, past, present and future. But we will not be free from the *presence* of sin until we leave our physical bodies and enter heaven.

Learning how to handle temptation and avoid sin is critical for a new believer. We must teach our young disciples to expect temptation and assure them that God can keep them from making sinful choices.

According to the scriptures below, what do you learn about the believer, sin, and temptation?

1 Peter 1:14-16

_____

_____

_____

1 John 1:6-10

_____

_____

_____

1 Corinthians 10:13

_____

_____

_____

Psalm 119:9-11

_____

_____

_____

## A New Believer Must Learn to Share the Gospel

When we receive good news, we love to share it! Just look at the success of social media. We love to tell others about the good things going on in our lives. New believers are often the most effective witnesses for Christ, because the excitement and joy of what God has done for them is fresh and real. As we disciple new believers, we should encourage them to begin sharing their story with others immediately. It should become a natural part of their conversations.

According to each scripture below, why is it important for us to know how to share the gospel?

Romans 1:16

_____
_____
_____
_____

2 Corinthians 5:18-20

_____
_____
_____
_____

2 Timothy 2:23-26

_____
_____
_____
_____

1 Peter 3:15

_____
_____
_____
_____

Loving others begins with getting to know our new family. A new believer may feel as though they have been transported to a foreign country. There is a new language to learn, new habits and customs. As we fellowship with other believers, we begin to feel at home in our new family. We develop relationships that challenge us, love us, and keep us accountable in our walk with Christ. As we learn to handle temptation and obey God, our lives begin to take on Christ-likeness. We love others by treating them as Christ would. This flows over into our relationships with unbelievers, as we develop a heart of compassion for those who do not know Christ.

\*\*\*

Our purpose in discipling a new believer is to **give them roots** or **ground them in the faith.** It is best to choose a simple curriculum to guide you through this process. The topics we've looked at in learning how to love God and love others are covered in *One-to-One Discipling*, a highly-recommended resource from Multiplication Ministries (see Appendix for source). Whatever curriculum you choose, here are a few guidelines to consider:

1. Choose a curriculum that is scripture based. The greatest gift you can give to a new believer is an excitement for and an understanding of God's Word. A simple format of looking up scripture and writing down observations is best.

2. Choose a curriculum that has daily homework, followed by a weekly time of discussion between mentor and disciple. A new disciple needs to learn directly from God's Word, but also needs encouragement and direction in application and understanding.

3. Choose a curriculum that requires an adequate length of time together, as it takes time to develop relationships. Be committed to spending enough time together to result in honest, open discussions. You want to see evidences of true spiritual growth and continuing maturity before releasing your disciple.

4. Choose a curriculum that covers the basics of who God is, how we respond to Him, and how we live a life of obedience.

**We believe the study you hold in your hand is a great place to begin with a new believer. Your excitement in learning to share the gospel will be a great foundation to help them grow and become disciple-makers themselves.** In the back of this study, you will find a list of other resources to consider as you commit to leading a new believer through the first steps of his new life in Christ.

As you end this week's study, pray a prayer of commitment to be used by God to disciple another believer. If you do not feel comfortable yet in leading someone else, pray about being discipled yourself, so that you grow into maturity, ready to lead others.

[1] Exponential [Blog]. *Discipleship Is: 70 Leaders on Discipleship.* (2013)
https://exponential.org/discipleship-is-40-leaders-on-discipleship/.
[2] Platt, David. *Radical: Taking Back Your Faith From The American Dream.* (Colorado: Multnomah Books, 2010), 181.

# Chapter Six
## Equipping New Believers for Ministry: His Church

*And He put all things in subjection under His feet,*
*and gave Him as head over all things to the church,*
*which is His body, the fullness of Him who fills all in all.*
Ephesians 1:22-23

### Day 1 – What is the Church?

As we've journeyed through scripture over the past five weeks, we've had an end in mind. The goal of *Going Around The Corner* is not just to gain biblical knowledge or enjoy fellowship in God's Word with a group of believers, although those are excellent and worthy endeavors. The end goal of our study is that we are challenged to reproduce – to see new believers birthed into the kingdom of God.

We've learned what it means to *explore* our neighborhoods, asking God to connect us with other Christ-followers and give us a heart of compassion to pray for our neighbors. We've committed to *engage* our neighbors by prayer walking, listening to the prompting of the Spirit, and reaching out through biblical good works – caring for our neighbors. We've accepted the call to *evangelize*, learning how to engage people of peace in spiritual conversations, share our own story, and present the gospel.

Last week we moved to a new level – how to begin discipling a new believer, to *establish* them in their faith. Establishing a believer is laying a firm foundation of biblical understanding of the basics of the Christian life. If we compare it to building a house, we have poured the foundation and put up the framing. Now we must move to the interior furnishing of the house – we must *equip* the believer to fulfill his or her role in the kingdom work of God. This happens by connection with a local church body.

According to Ephesians 1:22-23, what is the church?

_____
_____
_____


Who fills the church?

_____
_____

Who is the head of the church?

_____

_____


Throughout the New Testament, God uses the picture of a physical body to help us understand the spiritual body of Christ – the church. When a person comes to salvation, they become part of the universal church, the body of Christ. Beyond denominations, church buildings, theology, liturgy, and man-made traditions, the body of Christ is a spiritual entity.

Read Ephesians 2:11-16.

How was the body of Christ formed?

_____

_____

_____


What was the enmity that Christ abolished?

_____

_____

_____


What did the cross accomplish?

_____

_____

_____


The death of Christ on the cross reconciled us to God. There is no longer a wall of broken commands between us and God – by the blood of Jesus, that wall was removed, and we are now at peace with God. In reconciling both Jews and Gentiles to Himself, God formed a new body – a spiritual group of redeemed humans, united by the Spirit of God and led by the Head, Christ. If you are a Christ-follower, one who has been saved by the blood of Christ, you are part of that body.

A new believer needs to understand that they are now part of something wonderful! The body of Christ.

Read Ephesians 2:19-22. What words does Paul use to describe the body of Christ?

_____

_____

_____

Who is the cornerstone?

_____

_____

What do you think Paul means when he says we are being "fitted together" and "built together"?

_____

_____

Who dwells in this "holy temple" of united believers?

_____

_____

According to 1 Peter 2:4-6, what are believers called?

_____

_____

Here we have another beautiful picture of the body of Christ – a holy temple, or a building. We see Christ Himself as the cornerstone. A cornerstone is the first and most important stone set in the construction of a masonry foundation. It is important, because all other stones are set in reference to this stone. Just as a physical cornerstone ties the walls together at the corner, Jesus is the center reference point between the Old Testament (the Jewish law and the prophets) and the New Testament (the apostles). A church is not a true, biblical church, unless it centers in Jesus.

What is the church?

- The church is a spiritual body, made up of gifted individuals with Jesus as its head.
- The church is a spiritual building, made up of individual living stones, with Jesus as its cornerstone.

How does the universal church, the spiritual body of Christ, accomplish its purpose?

The body of Christ is manifested in the local church body – the group of individuals meeting in community together in a specific location.

As a child, did you own a kaleidoscope? I thought they were the most amazing things. You pointed the end towards the light, and as you turned the cylinder, the most beautiful and interesting pictures would appear. To me, this is a great illustration of the church. The members of the body are like the pieces of mirror and glass in the kaleidoscope. Separately, we aren't very special. But when we are pointed toward the Light, Christ, and we come together as a local church, just as each piece slides into place when you turn the cylinder, a beautiful picture emerges. Each picture is different, just as each local body has its own personality and giftedness. But we are all parts of the whole – the beautiful kaleidoscope of the body of Christ.

**It is in the local church body that the spiritual body of Christ becomes visible**.

Read Ephesians 4:11-16.

List the five roles, or functions mentioned in verse 11.

_____

_____

_____

_____

_____

For what purpose did God give these functions (gifts)? (v. 12)

_____

_____

_____

What is to be the result of saints who are equipped? (v. 13)

_____

_____

_____

What is the contrast described in verses 14-16?

_____

_____

_____

How does a person move from being an unstable child to a mature man?

_____

_____

_____

How does the whole body work? What must take place?

_____

_____

_____

What is the "measure" of a mature man?

_____
_____
_____
_____

This passage is a wonderful explanation of how the church functions. The goal of a believer is to grow up into maturity – into Christ-likeness. Apostles, prophets, evangelists, pastors and teachers are gifted by the Spirit to carry out their ministry. The original twelve apostles established the New Testament church. Today, men and women are likewise gifted to carry on the work of establishing and equipping believers in the local church.

We are given six specific results of a saint who is properly equipped.

- An equipped saint carries out the work of ministry or service.
- An equipped saint strives to attain unity of the faith.
- An equipped saint grows in his knowledge of Christ.
- An equipped saint is mature and Christ-like.
- An equipped saint is doctrinally stable.
- An equipped saint loves the members of the body.

The local church is where a saint can be fully furnished or equipped. For a new believer, it is vital for their maturity in Christ to find a local church body in which to function as a part of the body of Christ. There, they will discover what it truly means to be a Christ-follower.

For the rest of this week, we will discover what scripture says about the role of the local church in the life of the individual believer, and how we can encourage others by carrying out our part in the body of Christ. Spend some time in prayer thanking God for your local church body.


**Day 2 – Equipped by the Spirit**

*God's glory is most majestically displayed not through you or through me, but through **us**. God raises up the Church, and says to all Creation in the heavens, on the Earth, and under the Earth, "This is the bride and body of My Son, bought and purchased by His blood to be My people and receive My power, and enjoy My presence, and declare My praise forever and ever."*
— David Platt[1]

Read Ephesians 3:10, and 3:20-21. List the purposes of the church you see in these verses.

_____
_____
_____
_____

These verses speak of "the power that works within us." What does this mean?

Look up the following scriptures and explain this concept.

Ephesians 1:13-14
Ephesians 4:30
2 Corinthians 1:21-22
1 Corinthians 6:19

_____
_____
_____
_____
_____
_____
_____
_____

As believers, we are given the Holy Spirit as a pledge, or guarantee of our inheritance. When we die, we will enter the presence of God and know Him fully, but until then, we have the incredible blessing of the indwelling Spirit to guide us into Christlikeness.

As we see in Ephesians 3, the purpose of the church is to display the wisdom and glory of God in this world – both to the unseen spiritual world (rulers and authorities in heavenly places), and to the physical world we live in (all generations). This can only happen as the Spirit of God lives out the life of Christ in us.

According to 1 Peter 4:10-11, how is God glorified?

_____
_____
_____

Every believer possesses one or more spiritual gifts. These gifts are given by God intentionally and specifically to the individual believer, for the purpose of bringing Him glory, and to serve one another. The local church is the place where spiritual gifts are discovered, developed, and used to bring glory to God and accomplish His purposes.

Read 1 Peter 4:10 again. How are we to employ our gifts?

_____

_____

There are two primary passages in scripture that have much to teach us about spiritual gifts. Let's examine both.

Read Romans 12:1-8 and answer the following questions.

What is the believer's spiritual service of worship? What are we to do?

_____

_____

_____

How are we to think of ourselves, in relation to the members of the body?

_____

_____

How many members are there?

_____

_____

How many bodies?

_____

_____

How are the members of the body of Christ the same?

_____

_____

How are the members of the body different?

_____

_____

What differs, according to the grace given to us?

_____

_____

_____

List the different gifts you find in this passage (there are seven).

_____

_____

_____

_____

_____

_____

_____

This passage teaches us that we are all connected to one another as believers, because we belong to one body, the body of Christ. As members of the body, we are individuals, having different functions and differing gifts. These gifts are given "according to grace." In other words, we did nothing to earn or merit the gift, and each gift is equally important.

Read 1 Corinthians 12:4-31 and answer the following questions.

Fill in the blanks, according to verses 4-6:

There are varieties of _____, but the same _____.
There are varieties of _____, but the same _____.
There are varieties of _____, but the same _____.

Here we see that spiritual gifts are not just about the work of the Holy Spirit. The entire Godhead, the Trinity, is involved!

Gifts have their source in the Spirit. The Spirit gives us the **power** to accomplish the work of the church. Ministries are the **presence** of Christ in the world, as the church serves as His hands and feet, ministering in His name. The resulting effects accomplish the **purpose** of a Sovereign God, working out His plans through the body of Christ: reaching the world with the gospel, manifesting the glory and wisdom of God.

According to verse 7, why do gifts manifest the Spirit?

_____

_____

_____

Read verses 11 and 18. Who distributes the gifts?

_____

_____

_____

What two phrases are used in verses 11 and 18?

Just as _____

Just as _____

According to verses 14-26, which members of the body are the most important? Which members are unimportant, or less important?

_____
_____
_____

Why does God say there should be no division among the members (division meaning that one considers himself more important than another)? What should happen instead? (v. 25-26)

_____
_____
_____
_____

Referencing verses 8-10 and 28-30, list some of the spiritual gifts, ministries and effects mentioned in this chapter.

_____
_____
_____
_____

Discovering and using our spiritual gifts takes place within the context of the local church body. This is a crucial part of a new believer's growth to maturity – to understand that the Spirit of God lives in him and has specifically and intentionally gifted and equipped him to serve as part of the body.

Have you discovered your own spiritual gifts? If you don't know how God has gifted you, talk to your pastor or Bible study leader. They will help you discover your gifts and will be happy to put you in a place to serve. We've also listed some resources for you in the appendix of this study.

If you know your gifts, write them here, then spend time in prayer asking God to show you how He desires to use your gifts to serve your local church body, and bring Him glory.

_____
_____
_____
_____

## Day 3 – Equipped by Community (Part 1)

*And they were continually devoting themselves to the apostles' teaching and to fellowship, to the breaking of bread and to prayer.*
Acts 2:42

The birth of the early church was a dramatic experience. After His resurrection, Jesus spent 40 days on earth before His ascension and return to heaven. During that time, He appeared to many people, giving irrefutable proof that He truly conquered death and was alive. He met with the disciples, encouraging and teaching them. Then He gave His final instructions.

Look up Matthew 28:19-20 and Acts 1:4-8. What specific commands did Jesus give before He left?

_____
_____
_____
_____
_____

Jesus left the disciples with a great task (go into the world and make disciples) and promised they would be equipped for that task (the Holy Spirit would come to "baptize" or indwell them). This happened in Acts 2 in a very visible and spectacular way. The church, the body of Christ on earth, was born!

How did the disciples respond? As they began to gather in local house churches, what did "church" look like?

Read Acts 2:41-47.

What was the first thing that new converts did, after receiving the word of salvation?

_____
_____

To what were the believers devoted?

_____
_____

How did they treat one another?

_____
_____
_____

How did they spend their time?

_____

_____

_____

What was their attitude?

_____

_____

_____

What was the result for the church?

_____

_____

_____

This passage of scripture reveals six key ways that the local church *equips* a new believer through *community*.

A new believer needs to be baptized.
A new believer needs to celebrate communion.
A new believer needs to be taught the word of God.
A new believer needs to fellowship with other believers.
A new believer needs to pray.
A new believer needs to learn to share.

Let's see what scripture can teach us about each of these important principles, and how they take place in the context of a local church.

**Baptism & Communion**

Baptism and communion are commonly known as "ordinances." The word simply means a rite or ceremony that is believed to be ordained, in this case, by God. We understand ceremonies. If you attend any public function that is a gathering for a specific cause or commonality, there will probably be ceremonial traditions. For instance, we all expect the national anthem to be played before the ball game. At a school function, we recite the pledge of allegiance. If we attend a wedding, we will see a "ring" ceremony, or a "unity candle" ceremony. A military function or high school graduation may include a presenting of the colors. At a funeral for a veteran, we might hear taps played.

Ceremonies are simply a way to remember and proclaim a common belief. They unite us. They stir our hearts and cause us to think about important things.

Jesus left the church two sacraments, or ordinances: baptism and communion. What do they mean?

According to Matthew 28:19-20, who commanded that new disciples are to be baptized?

_____

Baptism as a Christ-follower has a deep significance. We first see baptism in the New Testament in the ministry of John the Baptist. According to Mark 1:4, what kind of baptism did John the Baptist teach?

_____

_____

Read Acts 19:1-5. What do you learn about John's baptism, in contrast to the baptism of the apostles after Christ had risen and returned to heaven?

_____

_____

_____

_____

_____

_____

What kind of baptism is described in 1 Corinthians 12:13?

_____

_____

John's baptism was a picture looking **forward** to Christ, a baptism which indicated a person had repented of their sins. Paul taught the believers at Ephesus that they needed to be baptized in the name of Christ, a picture of the complete work of salvation. I Corinthians 12 tells us that at salvation, we are baptized into the Spirit of God. Baptism is, therefore, a physical picture of a spiritual event, in all cases.

According to Romans 6:3-4, how is physical water baptism a picture of salvation?

_____

_____

_____

Baptism illustrates the death, burial and resurrection of Jesus. We are laid back in the water (death), submerged (burial) and brought out of the water (resurrection). By participating in baptism, we are publicly proclaiming that salvation has been accomplished. It does not save us, and it is not a requirement for salvation. It is an act of obedience by a believer – a remembrance of what Christ has done and proclaiming it effective in our life. It is a way of identifying ourselves with Christ, who also was baptized as our example (Matthew 3:13-17).

Acts 2:42 speaks of the "breaking of bread." This is a reference to participating in communion, or a sharing in the Lord's supper.

According to Matthew 26:26-29, where did the practice of communion originate? What was the occasion?

_____

_____

_____


On the last night before His death, Jesus celebrated the Passover meal with His disciples. It was an intimate time together, one which Jesus Himself said He had earnestly desired to eat with them before His suffering began (Luke 22:15). Communion is special to a believer because it causes us to stop and remember the sacrifice our Savior made for us. Jesus gave the elements of Passover, the bread and the cup, special significance, and proclaimed the new covenant He would make between God and man by His death.

The meaning of communion could be studied extensively, but here we will look at one passage to understand its importance in the life of a new believer.

Read 1 Corinthians 11:23-28.

What does the bread represent in communion?

_____

_____

What does the cup (wine or juice) represent?

_____

_____

What are we proclaiming when we celebrate communion?

_____

_____

According to verses 27-28, what is important to remember when celebrating communion? What should take place before we participate?

_____

_____

Communion reminds us that Jesus' body was broken on the cross, and that His blood was shed for the forgiveness of our sins. It causes us to examine our heart and mind, confessing any known sin or disobedience before participating. It is an important part of a believer's spiritual life, as we never want to forget what Jesus did for us. It keeps us in communion with Him.

Baptism and communion are an important part of our spiritual life. As a new believer becomes a part of a local church body, they will be able to proclaim publicly the new life Christ has given them, through baptism, and they will begin to experience a growing intimacy with Christ, and an understanding of holiness, through celebrating communion.

Have you been baptized?
Are you celebrating communion as part of your spiritual journey?

If not, talk to your pastor about making your profession of faith public today!


### Day 4 – Equipped by Community (Part 2)

Yesterday we began exploring the six key ways that the local church *equips* a new believer through *community*, based on Acts 2:41-47:

A new believer needs to be baptized.
A new believer needs to celebrate communion.
A new believer needs to be taught the word of God.
A new believer needs to fellowship with other believers.
A new believer needs to pray.
A new believer needs to learn to share.

We discovered that baptism and communion are important ordinances that are given to the local church to celebrate, because they keep us grounded in our *salvation*. The remaining four have much to do with the *sanctification* process of a believer.

According to Ephesians 4:13, what is the goal of the believer?

_____
_____


Salvation begins a life-long process of sanctification, a becoming like Christ, or a maturing. The word "sanctification" means holiness. It is being "set apart." It is the work of the Holy Spirit in us, the outward evidence of the inward change that salvation has made.

Our sanctification takes place within the body of Christ. Think about how our physical body works together. Modern medicine has revealed how each system in our body relies on the other to work properly and maintain good health. The cardiovascular system works in conjunction with the respiratory system. Our immune system and endocrine system work together. Our muscular and skeletal systems work in tandem. And these are just a few of the many ways our human body works.

In the same way, the body of Christ is dependent on each member to achieve *spiritual health*, or sanctification, of each believer.

## Teaching of the Word

The Word of God is our source of truth. A believer cannot be a growing, maturing saint without spending time reading, meditating, hearing and studying God's Word.

According to 2 Timothy 3:16-17, who wrote scripture?

_____

List the four things for which God's Word is useful.

_____
_____
_____
_____

What is the end goal of God's Word?

_____
_____

2 Timothy 3:16 illustrates the value of the Word of God:

- The Word teaches – it shows us the correct path.
- The Word reproves – it shows us where we got off the path.
- The Word corrects – it shows us how to get back on the path.
- The Word trains – it shows us how to stay on the path.

What is our responsibility to the Word of God, according to 2 Timothy 2:15?

_____
_____
_____

According to each scripture, what are some other benefits of being taught God's Word?

Ephesians 4:14 and 5:6

_____

_____

_____

Colossians 2:8

_____

_____

_____

Hebrews 4:12

_____

_____

_____

Hebrews 5:11-14

_____

_____

_____

1 Peter 2:2

_____

_____

_____

1 Timothy 1:3-5

_____

_____

_____

We cannot emphasize enough the importance of God's Word to a new believer. The world has much to offer in the area of "spirituality" but very little substance in truth. As you lead a person to Christ and commit to establishing and equipping them in their faith, make much of the Word of God.

**Fellowship With Other Believers**

The word "fellowship" is the Greek word *koinonia*, and it means "to share in, participation." Imagine you were a believer in the days of the early church. As a Jew, you would be considered a blasphemer and a heretic. You would be persecuted, whether from losing business in your family trade, or to the extreme case of being thrown to the lions. I believe the early church understood true fellowship. They literally depended on one another for their food, physical protection, and spiritual encouragement.

According to Acts 2:44-46, what evidences do you see that they understood fellowship?

_____

_____

_____

Our American culture is one of independence, but the early church realized that inter-dependence, depending on one another, serving one another, caring for one another's needs, and holding each other accountable was the way the body of Christ was intended to function.

Look up each scripture. What do you learn about living in fellowship with other believers?

Proverbs 27:17

_____

_____

_____

Galatians 6:1-2

_____

_____

_____

Ephesians 4:25

_____

_____

_____

1 John 1:6-7

_____

_____

_____

Philippians 2:1-4

_____

_____

Hebrews 10:24-25

_____

_____

_____

Colossians 3:12-15

_____

_____

_____

Fellowship is important for many reasons.  We need encouragement and accountability to live holy lives.  We learn to care for and love one another as we participate in a local body.  We exercise our spiritual gifts in fellowship with one another.  Fellowship also protects us from the enemy.  Satan desires to steal, kill and destroy the believer (John 10:10).  By committing to being in fellowship with other believers, we are following the example of the early church and fulfilling one of God's purpose for the body.


**Learning To Pray**

Salvation begins with a prayer.  To pray is simply to communicate with God.  It can be verbal or within our heart.  We may pray when we are alone, or in a crowd.  Prayer is lifting up our concerns, our praise, and our adoration to God.

A new believer must learn to pray.  Just as with any spiritual discipline, we learn first by observing others, then participating.  In the local church body, a new believer will learn to pray in small groups, or by meeting one on one, or in large group settings.  As they listen to the prayers of others, and participate themselves, they will learn to pray.

According to 1 Thessalonians 5:17, how often should we pray?

_____

_____

Look up each scripture below and write down what you learn about prayer.


James 5:13-18

_____

_____

_____

_____

Matthew 6:5-6

_____

_____

_____

_____

Luke 5:16

_____

_____

_____

_____

Romans 8:26

_____

_____

_____

_____

Ephesians 6:18

_____

_____

_____

_____

Philippians 4:6

_____

_____

_____

_____

Colossians 4:2-3

_____

_____

_____

_____

1 Timothy 2:1-2

_____

_____

_____

_____

Revelation 5:8

_____

_____

_____

_____

Just as a parent loves to speak with their child, God loves to hear our prayers. He speaks to us in His Word, and we communicate with Him through prayer. Helping a new believer see the importance of prayer and encouraging them to develop a rich and vibrant prayer life is a key part of their spiritual growth.

## Learning To Share

*Do you not know that God entrusted you with that money (all above what buys necessities for your families) to feed the hungry, to clothe the naked, to help the stranger, the widow, the fatherless; and, indeed, as far as it will go, to relieve the wants of all mankind? How can you, how dare you, defraud the Lord, by applying it to any other purpose?*
- John Wesley[2]

Read Acts 2:44-45. Describe the generosity of the early church. What was their motivation?

_____

_____

_____

The believers in Acts 2 were motivated by needs. They no longer saw themselves as separate individuals, but as members of one body. Therefore, the needs of the body were met as a natural response.

According to 1 Corinthians 12:20-26, how are we to respond to the needs of the body?

_____

_____

_____

Read each scripture below and write down what you learn about generosity and sharing within the body of Christ. Look for the practical application.

Galatians 6:10

_____

_____

_____

Acts 20:33-35

_____
_____
_____

Matthew 6:1-4

_____
_____
_____

James 1:27

_____
_____
_____

James 2:15-16

_____
_____
_____

Hebrews 13:1-3

_____
_____
_____

Hebrews 13:5

_____
_____
_____

1 Timothy 6:7-11

_____
_____
_____

When we come to Christ, we learn new ways of thinking. Our priorities should change because our desires change. The more we learn of Christ, the more we start to think of others rather than ourselves. As a new believer becomes part of the body of Christ, connected to a local church body, they will learn not only to give of themselves in service but also how to share the resources of their time and money for the greater purposes of the kingdom of God.

Think about the four areas you learned about today: teaching of the Word, fellowship with other believers, prayer and practicing generosity. How are you doing personally in each of these areas? Are you consistently studying God's Word? Do you spend time with other believers? Is prayer a priority in your day? Are you willing to share your resources to meet kingdom needs?

Write a prayer to God confessing any area where you feel you might have failed to be completely committed to the purposes of the body of Christ. Then thank Him for renewing your heart to love and serve as Christ loved us.

_____

_____

_____

_____


### Day 5 – Equipped to Worship

> *Missions is not the ultimate goal of the church. Worship is.*
> *Missions exists because worship doesn't.*
> -- John Piper[3]

We have come to the final day of our study. Over the last six weeks we have been on a journey to discover how we can join in the Great Commission of Christ by intentionally reaching and teaching in our own neighborhoods.

We learned what it means to **explore** our neighborhood by accepting the call to the mission and asking God to bring other believers to help in this endeavor. We are committed to **engage** our neighbors by prayer walking and reaching out through biblical good works, caring for and sharing life with our neighbors. We have challenged ourselves to **evangelize** by sharing our story of salvation and asking God for opportunities to speak the gospel boldly. We understand what a new believer needs, by **establishing** them in their faith through personal discipleship, and encouraging them to be **equipped** as a member of the body in a local church.

As you step away from this study, our prayer is that you have been challenged and motivated by the Word of God to view where you live as your assigned mission field. You are on mission. You are sent by God to the place where He has called you to live. There are people living near you, working with you, and spending time in leisure activities with you whom God desires to hear the good news of Jesus Christ.

Is John Piper correct in the quote above?

Read Revelation 7:9-12.

In your own words, describe the scene in this passage.

_____
_____
_____
_____
_____
_____
_____

Do you agree that worship is the ultimate goal of the church? Why or why not?

_____
_____
_____
_____
_____

What does it mean to worship God?

To worship is to show homage or reverence. The word has the literal meaning to prostrate oneself, to lay down in adoration before the object of our worship. Commitment to missions is an act of worship. It is being willing to lay down our desires, our wants, our needs, and our agenda to reach the lost for Christ. Our act of worship is to invite the unbeliever to join us in worshipping God.

We worship God when we pray for our neighbors.
We worship God when we serve our neighbors.
We worship God when we speak the gospel to our neighbors.
We worship God when we help strengthen a new believer.
We worship God when we mature in our own faith.
We worship God when we bring others to our local church body, where they worship God with us.

Read each scripture below and note what you learn about worshipping God.

Psalm 86:8-10

_____
_____
_____

John 4:24

_____
_____
_____

Romans 12:1

_____
_____
_____

Revelation 15:3-4

_____
_____
_____

In the end, God will be worshipped by all nations.  But for those who reject Him, their recognition of Him will come too late.

According to Revelation 20:11-15, what happens to the individual who never responds to God's invitation of salvation?

_____
_____

To worship God is to understand His heart for the lost.  According to each scripture below, what does God desire?

1 Timothy 2:3-4

_____
_____
_____

John 3:16

_____
_____
_____

2 Peter 3:9

_____
_____
_____

As we close our study, consider this quote from John Piper:

*God is pursuing with omnipotent passion a worldwide purpose of gathering joyful worshippers for Himself from every tribe and tongue and people and nation. He has an inexhaustible enthusiasm for the supremacy of His name among the nations. Therefore, let us bring our affections into line with His, and, for the sake of His name, let us renounce the quest for worldly comforts and join His global purpose.*
-- John Piper[4]

Write a prayer of commitment to God expressing your heart to live on mission in your own neighborhood. Ask Him to give you a heart of love and compassion for the lost, and a passion to worship the Most High God with your life. Commit your life to be an act of worship, for Him and Him alone.

_____

_____

_____

_____

_____

_____

_____

_____

_____

_____

_____

_____

_____

_____

[1] Platt, David. *Follow Me: A Call To Live, A Call To Die.* (Illinois: Tyndale House Publishers, 2013), 173.
[2] Wesley Center Online. "On The Dangers Of Increasing Riches." *The Sermons Of John Wesley-Sermon 126,* http://wesley.nnu.edu/john-wesley/the-sermons-of-john-wesley-1872-edition/sermon-126-on-the-danger-of-increasing-riches/.
[3] Piper, John. *Let The Nations Be Glad! The Supremacy of God in Missions.* (Michigan: Baker Academic, Baker Book House Company, 2004), 17.
[4] Piper, John. *Let The Nations Be Glad! The Supremacy of God in Missions.* (Michigan: Baker Academic, Baker Book House Company, 2004), 43.

# Take The Next Step

*The path of God-exalting joy will cost you your life. Jesus said, "Whoever loses his life for my sake and the gospel's will save it." In other words, it is better to lose your life than to waste it. If you live gladly to make others glad in God, your life will be hard, your risks will be high, and your joy will be full.*
-John Piper[1]

Thank you for completing this Bible study. We consider it an honor that you would take time to work through the material, and we pray that it has taught you, challenged you and motivated you. God has given us a personal passion to see our own precious neighbors meet Christ, and we pray that He is stirring this same desire in you.

So now what? Here are five practical steps you can take to implement to message of this study into your life today.

1. Commit to being on mission in your own neighborhood or workplace.
2. Pray specifically for God to reveal other believers in your community who will join with you.
3. Begin prayer walking, listening to God's Spirit as He speaks to you about your neighbors.
4. Act when God's Spirit prompts you. Begin serving and caring for your neighbors in practical, tangible ways.
5. Share the gospel as God gives you opportunities.

If this study has made an impact on your life, please let us know by contacting us through our website: www.aroundthecornerministries.org.

\*\*\*

*Around The Corner Ministries exists to take the gospel to every neighborhood in America. Our mission is to equip followers of Jesus to engage their neighborhoods and communities with the gospel of Jesus Christ.*

**Around The Corner Ministries** is a partner to the local church, designed to teach and train Christ-followers how to evangelize their neighborhoods, workplaces, and communities. The goal is to grow healthy local churches filled with mature believers who are comfortable and passionate about sharing their faith. If you would like more information on how our ministry can partner with your local church, please contact us.

---

[1] Piper, John. *Don't Waste Your Life.* (Illinois: Crossway, 2003), 10.

# APPENDIX

# Turning Conversations To The Gospel

Here's a simple strategy you can use when talking to people you don't know very well, or when picking up conversations with your neighbors, friends, or co-workers.

**Surface** questions lead to
    **Personal** questions, which lead to
        **Religious** questions, which lead to
            **Spiritual** questions, which lead to
                The **Gospel**!

## Surface Questions

When you first meet someone, we naturally ask "surface" questions. We are interested in discovering who they are, where they came from, and what they do for a living. Questions like:

Where are you from?
How long have you lived here?
Where were you born?
What do you do for a living?

Topics in this stage of conversation might include the weather, current events, sports, local happenings, or sharing information about your community or workplace. Remember, this is a *conversation*, not an interview. Offer information about yourself that will naturally open the door to asking questions. When we open up about ourselves, it initiates trust, and encourages others to share about themselves.

## Personal Questions

Personal questions begin to reveal who a person is, their opinions, thoughts, beliefs, desires, hopes, and dreams. Topics of conversation include family, childhood memories, what they are passionate about, hobbies and why they enjoy them, or how they became involved in them, music preferences, etc. Most people have something they do for relaxation, so a good question to ask is, "What do you do for fun?" As you discuss their work, hometown, or childhood, this will lead to more personal questions about those topics. It will also open the door for you to share personal things with them.

Here are some personal questions to get people talking about themselves, and to allow you to really get to know them on more than a surface level:

What are your hopes for your family, or yourself?

Who is your favorite musician?
What do you define as "family"?
Are you involved in any kind of community service?
Do you volunteer anywhere?
If you could live in a book, tv show, or movie, what would it be? Why?
How do you want to be remembered?
If you could travel anywhere, where would you like to go?
If you could speak another language, what would it be?
What teacher or mentor inspired you, and how?
What are you afraid of the most?

The goal of personal questions is to establish common ground. Be interested in their opinions and interest, even if they disagree with your own. The goal is to get to know the person and create a bond of trust where you can move to deeper, spiritual things. You are not trying to impose your ideas or opinions on them; you are trying to get to know theirs.

### Religious Questions

At this point, your goal is to begin moving the conversation toward the gospel. Religious questions are the next step. Religious questions allow us to engage a person's level of interest in spiritual topics.

A terrific transition question is "What do you like to do on the weekends?" After they respond, you can share what you do: (Example: "On Saturdays, we usually catch up on housework and yardwork, but Sundays are a rest day. We go to church in the morning and then eat lunch with family afterwards.") This provides an opening for your next question, "Do you attend church?"

From their answer, you will be able to tell if they are interested in talking about religious topics. If they do not attend church, but mention they went as a child, you can ask questions about their experiences as a child, and what they remembered about it.

Here are some other ideas for religious questions:

How do you celebrate Christmas? Easter?
Have you ever read the Bible?
What do you believe about heaven?
Do you pray?
What does prayer mean to you?

## Spiritual Questions

If your friend is still talking to you at this point, you can move into spiritual questions – topics that specifically talk about Jesus. Questions like "What do you believe about God?" or "What do you think about Jesus?" will give you a clear indication if they are ready to hear your story, and the gospel.

This is a great time to ask: "Would it be okay if I shared my story with you?" If they say yes, then briefly share how you became a Christian. As you tell your story, be sure to integrate the complete gospel. You want your story to be the catalyst to introducing them to the One who will change their life: Jesus.

## How To Become A Christ-Follower

Believe that God created you for a relationship with Him (believe).
Genesis 1:27 – *God created man in His own image, in the image of God He created him; male and female He created them.*
Colossians 1:16b – *All things have been created through Him and for Him.*

Recognize that you are separated from God (admit).
Romans 3:23 - *For all have sinned and fall short of the glory of God.*

Be willing to turn from your sin (repent).
1 John 1:9 – *If we confess our sins, He is faithful and righteous to forgive us our sins and to cleanse us from all unrighteousness.*

Believe that Jesus died on the cross and rose from the grave (accept).
Romans 10:9-10 – *That if you confess with your mouth Jesus as Lord, and believe in your heart that God raised Him from the dead; you will be saved; for with the heart a person believes, resulting in righteousness, and with the mouth he confesses, resulting in salvation.*

Invite Jesus in to control your life through the Holy Spirit (receive).
John 1:12 – *But as many as received Him, to them He gave the right to become children of God, even to those who believe in His name.*

## What To Pray

*Dear Jesus, I recognize that I am separated from You because of my personal sin, and I need Your forgiveness. I believe that You died on the cross to pay the penalty for my sin. I confess my sin and ask You to forgive me. By faith, I turn from my way of life to follow You instead and accept Your gift of salvation by grace. I ask You to come into my life and transform me. Thank You for saving me and giving me eternal life. Amen.*

# Additional Resources

aroundthecornerministries.org

### Going Around The Corner Bible Study, Student Edition
ISBN: 9780692781999 / List Price: $10.99
A five-session workbook covering the first four chapters of the original study for high school and college students with expanded commentary and practical application, focusing on reaching their campus, dorm, and playing field for Christ. Students will be guided into God's Word and develop an awareness and passion for sharing the gospel.

### Going Around The Corner Bible Study, Leader Guide
ISBN: 9780999131824
List Price: $3.99
Key truths for each week, helpful discussion starters and thoughtful questions to help your group apply the principles in the study, plus suggested group activities and practical application steps. Adaptable for use with the Student Edition.

### 40 Days of Spiritual Awareness
ISBN: 9780999131800 / List Price: $9.99
A 40-day devotional to understand who God is and how He is working in the people right around you. Each day, discover truth that will increase your awareness of God, yourself, other believers, and unbelievers. Be reminded of what is important: an awareness of God's work in our world, as He redeems and saves. At the end of the journey, you will realize that you are an important part of accomplishing that work, and be prepared to join Him.

### Living In Light of the Manger
ISBN: 9780999131817 / List Price $9.99
If the manger only has meaning during our holiday celebrations, we've missed the point of the story. Jesus was born, so that we could be *born again.* The events of His birth and the people who welcomed Him have many lessons to teach us about the glorious gospel and how Jesus came to change our lives. Discover the purpose and power of the manger through 40 daily devotions. Perfect to introduce the gospel to friends, co-workers and neighbors.

### Grace & Glory: A 50-Day Journey In The Purpose & Plan Of God
ISBN: 9780999131848 / List Price $11.99
What do we do when we face a crisis of faith? When everything we believe is challenged? That's when we must discover (or re-discover) God's purpose for our lives and learn to live with a mindset of His grace...grace that reveals His glory. This devotional will refresh believers in the gospel and encourage them to live every day so that the glory of God will be proclaimed by the power of grace at work in their lives.

**The following are resources from other ministries which are helpful in sharing the gospel, discipling new believers and growing your own faith.**

Follow Me: Becoming A Lifestyle Prayer Walker
*A Bible study that will transform a willing believer into an effective prayer walker.*
Randy Sprinkle, New Hope Publishers, Birmingham, AL
www.newhopepublishers.com

One-to-One Discipleship
*A nine-session course for one believer to help another believer learn the nine foundation stones upon which to build the rest of their lives.*
Al and Lorraine Broom, Multiplication Ministries, Vista, CA
www.multimin.com

Shine His Light
*A Simple Way to Pray, Care and Share Jesus in Your Neighborhood*
Alvin VanderGriend, Prayer Shop Publishing, Terre Haute, IN
www.prayershop.org

Be Jesus In Your Neighborhood
*Developing a Prayer, Care, Share Lifestyle in 30 Days*
Alvin VanderGriend, Prayer Shop Publishing, Terre Haute, IN
www.prayershop.org

The Knowledge of the Holy
*The Attributes of God: Their Meaning in the Christian Life*
A.W. Tozer, Harper Collins Publishers, New York, NY
www.harpercollins.com

I Am A Church Member
*Discovering the Attitude that Makes the Difference*
Thom S. Rainer, B&H Publishing, Nashville, TN
www.BHPublishingGroup.com

Gospel
*Recovering the Power that Made Christianity Revolutionary*
J.D. Greear, B&H Publishing, Nashville, TN
www.BHPublishingGroup.com

Share Jesus Without Fear
*Conquer your fears about sharing, build relationships with unbelievers and help new believers grow in their faith*
William Fay, B&H Publishing, Nashville, TN
www.BHPublishingGroup.com

## Additional Helps

Bless Every Home – an online community that sends daily reminders of your neighbors' names to pray for, along with suggested scriptures to pray. Sign up at https://blesseveryhome.com/.

Lewis, Casey. "Plow and Pursue: Turning A Conversation to the Gospel." *Christianity Matters*, October 16, 2012, www.christianitymatters.com/2012/10/16/plow-and-pursue-turning-a-conversation-to-the-gospel-part-1/

Schneider, Floyd. "How To Turn A Conversation To Spiritual Things." *Crosswalk*, October 3, 2001, www.crosswalk.com/faith/spiritual-life/how-to-turn-a-conversation-to-spiritual-things-900808.html

Reeves, Josh. "25 Simple Ways To Be Missional In Your Neighborhood." *Verge Network*, August 23, 2011, www.vergenetwork.org/2011/08/23/25-simple-ways-to-be-missional-in-your-neighborhood/

Ferguson, Dave. "Five Ways To Bless Your Neighbors." *Verge Network*, December 27, 2012, www.vergenetwork.org/2012/12/27/five-ways-to-bless-your-neighbors-dave-ferguson/

Life Conversation Guide: 3 Circles – A short conversation guide with visuals you can use to share the gospel. A Life On Mission Resource, North American Mission Board. Order at www.sendnetwork.com.

We invite you to visit **aroundthecornerministries.org** for more encouragement as we **go around the corner** together.

CPSIA information can be obtained
at www.ICGtesting.com
Printed in the USA
BVHW051202180821
614616BV00018B/1458

9 780692 781999